# A Love Affair
# With Vermont Weather

Merry Christmas &
Best wishes for 2008 Tracy!

Love, Kevin & Ellen

Three Historic Randolph Center homes where Vermont Weather has been tracked for almost 100 years.

# A Love Affair

# With Vermont Weather

## A Selection of "Weatherwise" Columns
## Published in the Herald of Randolph

**By Miriam Herwig**

**Edited and with an Introduction by
Kevin P. Doering**

A Love Affair
With Vermont Weather

A Selection of "Weatherwise" Columns
Published in the Herald of Randolph

First Edition

ISBN 0-9772615-4-9

Printed in the United States of America

# Table of Contents

*In loving memory of my husband, Wes Herwig,*
*who encouraged my writing in fair weather and foul*

*Also dedicated to the Editor's wife Ellen,*
*who by her continuing generosity of time and spirit*
*allowed me to complete this important local history*
*and meteorological project*

# *Introduction*

This book really began when our family moved to Randolph Center from Maine in the summer of 2002. After a difficult ordeal, during which our moving van had broken down the previous night, my wife was greeted by long time Center resident, historian and "Weatherwise" column writer Miriam "Mim" Herwig, bearing a welcoming gift of fresh picked raspberries from her garden. How could she know these were my wife's favorite fruit? Mim is a gentle lady who always seems to be in the right place at the right time here in the Center, serving others when not recording history, nature and weather with her long-time husband and fellow historian, Wes Herwig. It wasn't long before we were guests at their comfortable home learning about local history and of course engaging in discussions about Vermont weather.

Coincidentally, while Mim was recording weather here in the Center and faithfully writing her weekly column for the "Herald of Randolph," I had been recording weather daily for over 25 years in northeastern locations ranging from New Jersey to Maine. I had started taking observations as a boy living in central New Jersey. My parents gave me my first weather station, for Christmas, when I was 11, and I faithfully recorded daily temperature, wind speed estimates and barometric pressure at our home. I can recall that the thermometer was positioned outside my bedroom window, where in the late afternoon the western sun would strike, often forcing me to estimate the "real" or shade temperature. I also recall a strong love for snow inherited from my mother, who used to draw pictures for me of homes surrounded by piling snow and wind driven drifts always accompanied by the spiral of smoke emanating from the chimney. Since there wasn't enough snow in New Jersey to satisfy me, I would hoard it by shoveling what fell into piles, storing it in shady, covered locations. I would later amaze my friends when a snowball would come seemingly out of nowhere from a landscape which, even in winter, hadn't seen snow for weeks.

This longing for snow was destined to be fulfilled when my family moved to Maine in 1975. Winters took on additional significance and weather reporters were given twice the length of time to detail their forecasts. I made meteorology my career, majoring in the study of it at Rutgers University. It was at Cook College, the agricultural school of Rutgers, where I met my future wife, Ellen, also a meteorology major who had a love of things atmospheric, particularly the sky and clouds. I began my first full time job as a meteorologist for the Maine Department of Environmental Protection. I continued to take weather readings though we moved several times - this was just something that I needed to do daily.

Eventually, (and certainly not by accident), I landed a position in Vermont. We relocated to a home within the historic district of Randolph Center, which due to its hilltop location just east of the Green Mountains provides a full panoply of Vermont weather to both endure and enjoy. Our new location was like a dream come true for a family headed by one who loved snow and another who loved the sky. The snow season is longer here than in south-central Maine and the sunrises, sunsets and overall beauty experienced along the

Green Mountains are always changing and often spectacular. In addition, we found all the local amenities we had enjoyed in our town in Maine - a store to walk to, ski trails and a lake to enjoy. Adding to this was the keen sense of heritage which I felt pervaded the historic district here.

That history has been well chronicled by the Herwigs, in part through their forty books and their work in the local history museum. Of particular interest were the summaries on nature and weather compiled faithfully by Mim from 1978 through 2003, and recorded weekly in the Herald's column entitled "Weatherwise." The columns are a treasure trove of weather records and natural observations gleaned through the eyes of the poet and historian Mim from this hilltop central Vermont location. They continued a tradition begun back in 1829 by Squire William Nutting, who lived in a brick home almost across the street from the Herwigs' historic home and only a few buildings south of my home. Mr. Nutting left us a 34 year history of weather records faithfully compiled at the same times each day from 1829 to his death in 1863.

I also learned from Mim that our town has had residents recording weather basically uninterrupted back to the Nutting records. According to Mim the Hibbards, early settlers who lived on the Ridge road, also kept journals containing weather information beginning about 1860 for three generations. Unfortunately the last of the family took the journals to Massachusetts. Given these records, (which I hope to track down some future day) and Mim's journal entries, which go back long before the writing of the weekly "Weatherwise" column, it is certainly possible that the Center has a recorded atmospheric and natural history of more than 175 consecutive years. From a meteorological point of view they represent a significant repository of information and for example, could provide clues towards the often referenced cooling or warming periods frequently debated when discussing global climate change. Although the data is important, it represents only a fraction of the value of Mim's beautifully scripted page after page delivered to the Herald for 25 years. I hope to convey something of that value in the pages that follow.

Much of "Weatherwise" is expressed poetically, telling readers about the past week's weather and the ebb and flow of the natural scene surrounding her home. These reports were much more than weather; they depicted the natural elements and how we interact and are impacted by them. The changes of season are detailed along with how our lives are shaped by the natural world surrounding us. The gales of winter, the mud of early spring, the return of song birds and the greening of the land are eloquently described along with the sullen heat of summer and the dramatic coloring of the autumn landscape. Countless readers were enthralled by Mim's writing, and scores of them let the Herald and Mim know personally of their growing attachment to her column. There were many notes of regret when Mim decided to end the column, though her decision gave me the opportunity to continue it to the present time.

While I feel privileged to continue the tradition of "Weatherwise," I readily admit that I do not bring Mim's poetic or natural instincts to the week's review. This is another reason why I believed it is important to preserve some of her best writing in this book.

Although meteorological data continues to be collected and recorded here in the Center, Mim's accomplishment would be lost for most without the pages compiled herein.

In continuing my study of local and statewide weather, I have learned that I fortuitously arrived at a special place for tracking meteorological events. The weather here can be almost ferocious - Mim occasionally recorded hurricane-force winds (and not from hurricanes or their remnants either). The sky can change in minutes, but the location and openness of this unique hill top location often provide observers with "lead time" to notice upcoming changes. The Center also offers a wide expanse of sky, often touched by beautiful sunrises and sunsets so often noted within "Weatherwise." And the temperature is distinctive to the location, usually cooler than the surrounding valley but sometimes higher on the still bitter-cold mornings when the coldest air sinks to the lower elevations. Of course the Center is sometimes swept by winds which produce bone-chilling wind-chill factors. On such days Mim often noted the warmth of hearth and home. The 1384 foot elevation also produces conditions refreshingly cooler in the summer - thus historically attracting summer vacationers.

These columns give us a sense of the incredible variety of weather here and disclose how each month and season hold surprises for even the best of Vermonts' meteorologists. The accounts continue to fascinate, even in today's high-tech, satellite, and computer-driven society, and serve as backdrop for our daily conversations. Moreover, they give us an important glimpse of the author, a remarkable historian who has centered much of her life on a love of nature and weather.

Mim is the eternal optimist, evident in the darkest days of winter when you read of the growing length of day and of her eternal hope for spring. She, along with husband Wes (of the Winter Hater's club fame), also brought a wry sense of humor to these pages along with local history and weather lore. My hope is that I have been able to capture the best of these while also incorporating the full range of weather conditions that we "enjoy" here in Randolph Center.

When I approached Mim with the idea for this book she was warmly receptive and suggested that I limit its scope to one column a week for 52 columns in all. However, after 100 hours immersed in her scrapbooks, I concluded that such a limitation would not capture the essence of the more than 1,250 columns she wrote. With Mim's permission I have expanded this to include portions of hundreds of other columns. What you find in the following pages is a quarter century of Central Vermont weather, highlighted by pieces of poetry and meteorological and historic observations from Mim. These spell the essence of her remarkable writing during this period. My aim has been to provide the reader with the unending variety of weather by week and season, along with Mim's talented method of picturing it (and often our lives) here in this place she often refers to as the best little village in the whole world.

"One of the brightest gems in New England weather
is the dazzling uncertainty of it."
- Mark Twain

# January

JANUARY HOLDS MOST OF THE RECORDS FOR COLD BUT ALSO FEATURES THE JANUARY THAW, WHICH USUALLY ARRIVES IN THE THIRD OR FOURTH WEEK OF THE MONTH. ALL OF THIS IS DETAILED BY MIM WITH HER SIGHTING OF BIRDS AND OTHER SIGNS FROM THE QUIETEST TIME OF THE YEAR.

*January 1-7:*          *"Some say the world will end in fire,*
*Some say in ice"*
*And most of us were inclined to agree with [Robert] Frost's latter ending last Friday. Though the sun shone valiantly all day, temperatures steadily dropped below zero and the wind howled up a chill of -56 degrees!*

*The new year had begun bravely with a dazzlingly sunny day and temps warm enough to send snow crashing off roofs. But Tuesday was another matter. Brr! It stayed cold all day, and that night fluffy snow started falling without stopping, piling up 12 inches by Wednesday night.*

*Frigid conditions continued unabated through the weekend, bringing to our mind a saying of our stoic ancestor - "What can't be cured must be endured."*

*And enduring it we were, with a variety of complaints when cars would not start, ice backed up on roofs and traveling was precarious, whether pedestrian or vehicular.*

*The scene was monochromatic, for a good 18 inches of snow upholstered field and forest. Living under such conditions is undoubtedly character-building, but the type of character is questionable.*          1996

Also excerpted from the first week of 1988 (and summarizing the year just past):
*Events which stand out about the year just finished include a 51 inch snowfall in January, a second disastrous sugaring season, sweltering weather at the end of May, the first shower on the Fourth of July parade in its history, the hottest summer in 40 years, 8 inches of heavy, windblown snow causing much damage on Oct. 4, and 4 more inches of snow on Oct. 11.*

From the first week of 1989:
*Fifty-five years ago last Thursday the thermometer in Bloomfield, Vt. bottomed out at 50 degrees below zero, the coldest temperature ever recorded in the state. This observer can remember food freezing in our farmhouse cellar then, despite heat from a cast iron kettle filled with coals.*

1990:
*The serenity of the whitened countryside calls for a more deliberate pace, as the pulse of nature slows down. The stillness of January is good for reassessment and contemplation on the course of our lives.*

*While some creatures hibernate and others migrate to escape the rigors of winter, humans adapt to conditions like the recent extreme cold. The stark simplicity surrounding us is refreshing after the gaiety and bustle of the holidays.*

From 1998, on the major ice storm that the Center missed:

*Never in weather annals has there been a week like the past one, and let us hope there will never be another! Calamity of unheard of proportions struck areas north of us as continued freezing rain kept crashing down ice-coated limbs and power lines, leaving three million in Canada and at least 35,000 in Northern Vermont without power.[1]*

2002:

*January, according to a 150 year old chart of farm chores, was the time for visiting. Most friends and relatives were within the distance of a sleigh ride, and activities on the farm were at their lowest level. How beneficial to today's society would be a designated time for visiting!*

January 7-13:

*Last winter's lowest temperature of 14 degrees below zero hardly seems worth mentioning in the light of eleven mornings with vastly lower readings already this season.*

*With the temperature dropping well below zero every day but one last week, Vermonters are using every known trick to outwit the cold. There is an incomparable satisfaction in the cozy warmth of a family circle while blustery north winds blow outside.*

*Entrenched in our individual fortresses, we send up smoke signals declaring our readiness to do battle with the elements. This promises to be the winter we will tell our grandchildren about.*                                                                1981

From the second week of 1986:

*Snow crunched under foot as we shivered in the cold the first of last week....In the struggle for survival against the elements, a giant pileated woodpecker ransacked neighborhood maples in search of deep-hidden insects.*

1992:

*One hundred fifty years ago, William Nutting, a meticulous weather observer who lived in the brick house on the VTC campus, had logged 154 inches of snow the previous winter and was busy adding to what would be 98 inches that winter. But worse was to come! The next five years had amounts of 166, 169, 140,103 and 127 inches of snow. Observing that weather usually runs in cycles, we can only believe that similar conditions will occur again.*

1997:

*Brr! Last Wednesday the wind chill was 40 degrees below zero! Then on Friday more than 9 inches of snow fell, thudding off roofs to pile up formidably under windows.*

*But if you think this weather is rough, listen to what it was like 140 years ago. The coldest day of the century occurred in January 1857 and on January 6 it was so cold*

---

[1] Editors Note: Here is one striking anomaly of where south central Maine (where I was recording weather at the time) was cooler than in-land Vermont. We received all freezing rain and lost power for 10 days.

*that the overheated furnace in Vermont's statehouse ignited surrounding wood and the capitol went up in flames!*

January 13-19:

*In the continued below-zero weather of last week, the whole pulse of living slowed down. Keeping warm and fed were the prime objectives of our days, as the tentacles of bitter cold crept into our homes and our very beings.*

*A kinship was felt with the early pioneers who struggled with the elements for survival. Also, there was a desperate longing for moderation in the bone-chilling temperatures.*

*By the end of the week, thermometers had edged up to the zero mark. Fortunately, there had been no wind to speak of until Saturday, to drive the chill factor lower.*

*A salmon-colored sunrise brightened Wednesday morning while the nearly full moon was accompanied by Orion, the hunter across the night skies.* 1981

From Wes Herwig, 1981:

*Winter Haters Stirring Again -*

*Winter Haters Anonymous, which was organized in Randolph Center during the darkest days of winter in 1979, has surfaced again, holding meetings in the chilly homes of charter members.*

*The formation of a Florida chapter is the latest project of this growing under-cover organization. Frostbite kits, pocket flasks, mittens and earmuffs are being collected to send to fellow grumblers there.*

*Plans for a chartered bus trip to Canaan, Vermont, where a record low of 43 degrees below zero was reported last week, have been given the cold shoulder. Instead, members agreed to sponsor a showing of the film, "Nanook of the North," at a coming meeting.*

From the third week of 1979:

*One good thing about the weather is that it provides a mutual topic of conversation, a common enemy for everyone to protest about. In typical January style, the temperature didn't get up to zero on some days last week, while cutting winds made the wind-chill factor at least 45 degrees below zero. What sunshine we did have was pale and weak, and served only as visual encouragement.*

1982:

*Winter has become our mutual foe - to be conquered by heat at home and skill on the road. Filigrees of frost adorn our windows and smoke curls up from our battle stations. Let the faint-hearted flee - we will continue to resist the elements.*

1984:

*Individual snowflakes glittered on the surface like diamonds. It is no wonder that the world's first and foremost photographer of snowflakes was a Vermont boy![2] It is worth our time to observe a few of these exquisite creations on the sleeve of a dark coat.*

---

[2] Wilson "Snowflake" Bentley

**1994:**

*Below-zero temperatures on five days plus bitter winds combined to create horrendous wind chills....Nails hammered in over a century ago contracted and popped explosively on frigid nights, and there was a brittle creaking of old trees as the wind assailed them.*

*But such conditions are to be expected of January. True, we have endured a couple of 50-hour spells of below-zero weather, but there are spine-chilling memories of much worse times in the past. In January, 1968, the temp stayed below 0 degrees F for 150 hours, while in February 1979 we battled sub-zero temperatures for 230 consecutive hours. Now we are one week closer to spring.*

**1997:**

*We Vermonters are proud survivors, knowing that the green quickening of spring is our reward for enduring the slings and arrows of outrageous winter.*

**January 19 - 25**

*Our January thaw arrived at last on the nineteenth, the first day with temperatures up to the thawing point since Dec. 29! One of the most noticeable improvements was the proliferation of smiles as sun shone and snow melted.*

*Last week had run-of-the-mill weather for January, with all but one day starting out above zero. There was a dusting of snow on Friday and Saturday, but the amount on the ground is scanty for this time of year.*

*Almost every day had dazzling sunshine, and daylight lasts noticeably longer as we near the midpoint between winter solstice and vernal equinox.*

*This is a time for contemplation and restoration, for poring over seed catalogs and dreaming new dreams before the flurry of warm weather activity starts.*      1981

**From the fourth week of 1983:**

*More birds have been flocking to the feeders now that the ground is covered with snow. Mourning doves, cowbirds, pine grosbeaks and goldfinches have joined the regular visitors. After our previously snow-less winter, the crunch of snow underfoot was music to our ears. The serenity of the whitened countryside calls for a more deliberate pace, as the pulse of nature slows down.*

**1986:**

*A genuine January thaw finished off the week in style, to the delight of everyone. Eaves dripped busily, slicing neatly through deep snow. It was smiling weather, as the temperatures soared high in the fifties Saturday. Fog engulfed us on Sunday, penetrated by rain, but still it was well above the freezing point.*

1987:

*Eager for our bounty, a variety of hungry wildlife appeared next morning, including a tiny but fierce shrew, a huge voracious goshawk, a beautiful cardinal and small pine siskins, in addition to flocks of regular customers - blue jays, mourning doves, cowbirds and evening grosbeaks.*

1994: Winter Haters Organize:

*It has been rumored that the subversive group called Winter Haters Anonymous has reformed in the vicinity of Randolph Center. The group first formed in 1979, a landmark winter, but recent mild excuses for the season caused the organization to atrophy. Now the winter of 1993-94 has re-energized the worthy group.*

*Sworn to eternal vengeance against the forces of evil which block driveways with snow and cause tempers to boil, members have vowed to publicly burn postcards or any communications from erstwhile friends frolicking in such balmy climates as Florida, California or worse yet, Hawaii.*

*Overcome by the direness of their plight and enduring ever higher mountains of snow on all sides, members offer the symbol of their fraternity, a clenched fist shaken futilely against the continually falling snow.*

*With lowered earflaps and glaring eyes, winter haters meet to compare notes on the miseries inflicted by below zero temperatures, icy walks and leaking roofs. It is said that a collection is taken periodically for the unfortunate soul whose fuel bill is the highest for the three months of 1994.*

*As the wind howls around the eaves, the winter haters howl around the fireplace, raising glasses to the early end of winter. The winter haters' coat-of-arms features a snow lizard rampant on a field of white with two crossed snow shovels on the crest, indicating readiness to attack.*

*The motto, like the fraternity oath, is unprintable.*

January 26 - February 1

*What an astonishing array of weather there was last week! Monday was so warm and thawing that a robin's chirping would not have seemed out of place. A row of green day lily shoots along the house foundation must have felt spring beckoning.*

*On Tuesday the darker side of such amazing warmth showed up in mud! That beautiful ring around the moon foretold precipitation, but Wednesday was a time of waiting.*

*Then shades of Snowflake Bentley! Snow fell unceasingly all Thursday, piling up seven fluffy inches. During the night, freezing rain glazed the land, causing the closing of 350 schools Friday.*

*Saturday morning's sunshine revealed broken branches and twinkling ice shards all over a thick crust and perilously icy driveways. Even if an incautious groundhog did see his shadow, we knew that winter was just beginning, instead of spring being only six weeks away.*

2002

From the fifth week of 1979:

*Roadside snow banks are so high they muffle sound and obscure traffic. And still the white stuff continues to fall. Some of it even falls twice, cascading down from roofs to form ever-increasing mounds in front of windows. One consolation is the realization that it provides excellent insulation.*

*"Some say the world will end in fire, some say in ice," and with Robert Frost we are inclined to agree that "for destruction ice is also great and would suffice." Scientists as well as poets would have us believe that the world is cooling off.*

*And Vermont official records concur, revealing that snowfalls from 1900 to 1945 never reached 90 inches in a winter. However, of the past ten winters, nine have had 90 inches or more, while the record of 145 inches was set in 1970-1971. It appears that Vermont is not going to the dogs but to the polar bears!*

Yet read this from the end of January in 1989:

*Our hilltop is one of the few places where Mother Nature's weary bones have a decent white covering this winter. Row upon row of corn stubble protrudes from scanty snow in the valleys. Red stems of dogwood bushes provide a touch of color in an otherwise bleak landscape.*

*Evening grosbeaks, usually voracious all-winter visitors, have only been seen once, an indication that northern feeding grounds are satisfactorily warm for them this year... This unusual weather has been puzzling Vermonters accustomed to deep cold and snow in January, and it is hoped that the benefits outweigh possible future water shortages.*

And more on cold weather from the fifth week of 1991:

*Old Man Winter began his siege by cold with a popping of nails last Monday morning. From a balmy 38 degrees the day before, the mercury had dropped to hover around zero all day. The next two days were even worse as the population huddled within their fortifications, watching supplies of oil and wood go up in smoke.*

# February

FEBRUARY IS OFTEN THE MONTH OF THE HEAVIEST SNOW, AND MIM'S DESCRIPTION OF THE FOUR WINTRY WEEKS OF 1993 FLOWED SO WELL TOGETHER THAT I USED THEM ALL TO DEPICT THIS MONTH'S DOMINANT THEME. ONE CAN ALMOST FEEL THE DEPTH OF SNOW AS IT PILES UP OUTSIDE ONE'S WINDOWS WHILE READING THESE DESCRIPTIONS. YOU WILL ALSO NOTE HER ETERNAL OPTIMISM AS WELL AS HEARTFELT THANKS TO THE MEN WHO BATTLE THE ELEMENTS WITH SNOWPLOWS IN OUR PART OF THE WORLD.

*February 1-7:*

*In Vermont, nothing is certain but death and taxation - and winter! And last Monday was a prime example of winter at its worst. Bone-chilling winds, higher than any last year, caused wind chills of 50 degrees below, and worse.*

*The tentacles of cold relaxed briefly midweek, and eaves were dripping Friday, forming ranks of icicles. Then temperatures plummeted 54 degrees by next morning, with record cold predicted for Sunday, lower in valleys than on hilltops like ours. However, Sunday's reading of 24 degrees below zero was far less than we had experienced in the winter of 1980-81, when two days registered 34 degrees below and 18 days of January were below zero.*

*Birds huddled about in fluffed-out balls of feathers, and smoke signals issued defiantly from chimneys in the battle against Old Man Winter.*                1993

And more from the first week of February, which usually included observations about groundhogs and Candlemas Day, 1996:

*Our chief business last week seemed to be outwitting Old Man Winter with hot drinks, warm clothing and more logs on the fire.... Groundhog Day passed without incident, for no Vermont woodchuck has even been known to emerge from his lair on February 2, whether it was cloudy or sunny.*

*According to the old saying, we were at the midpoint of winter,*
*"Half the wood and half the hay,*
*Should be left by Candlemas Day" [Feb. 2]*

From 1999:

*Each day last week was as different as a litter of kittens. Monday began with a gorgeous sight - a flaming sunrise in the east and the full moon still in the western sky. Tuesday brought a day full of snow, followed by rain, and Wednesday was a time for making lopsided snowmen.*

*The temperature zoomed up into the forties, snow melted and it surely felt like spring. To paraphrase Patrick Henry, if this be winter, let us make the most of it!*

2000:

*The rainbow-like sighting of parhelia in Wednesday's morning sky was the highlight of last week's weather. This rare atmospheric phenomenon, known in the vernac-*

ular as sun dog, occurs when sunlight is refracted through moisture, in this case ice crystals. "Helios" means sun in Greek, and the vertical pillars of light visible here were part of the parhelic circle around the sun.

It didn't take a groundhog to foresee six more weeks of winter in Vermont. Near zero days and frozen pipes make us realize that winter was strengthening its hold on us.

On the other hand, we were fortified by the lengthening days, for sunshine is essential to our well-being.

February 8 - 14:

No doubt about it - we are in for a "good old-fashioned winter," with plenty of snow and cold. We are reminded of the years when cars sported bandannas on their aerials to indicate their presence behind monstrous snow banks. In the really old days, team bells and sleigh bells rang out warnings of approaching traffic around corners.

Nature's unpredictable cycles have not changed much over the years. There have been "open winters" in the past, as well as blizzards. And, for the record, the severest winter in U.S. history was in 1780, when even New England's salt-water harbors froze over!

Our past week has crunched along, with four sunny days nicely offsetting the weekend snowstorm, which settled even as it continued falling. Theoretically, winter is half over now. Will this snowy season mean a great sugaring season ahead? Only time will tell. 1993

From the second week of February, 1992:

Surviving the rigors of winter was the chief claim to fame in the life of one early settler, whose gravestone proclaims he was "one of the first that endured the inclemencies of winter in this town." In that respect we are all kindred spirits!

1994:

The below-zero snow crunched beneath our feet as winter stretched on into a marathon of endurance last week. By Sunday seventy-three inches of the white stuff had fallen, with winter little more than half over....

But on Saturday a new word had crept into our constricted, Arctic vocabulary - thawing! There was the sparkle of a thousand diamonds as the sun shone brilliantly all day. For a time at least, we could forget the rule of 30, which struck terror into those forced to work under such (arctic) conditions. Quite simply, it states: A 30-mph wind blowing when it's 30 below zero will freeze exposed flesh in 30 seconds.

From 1998, quoting a bitter cold day from 1979:

As stoical Vermonters, this (cold weather) was what we had been bracing ourselves for, and we felt quite capable of weathering whatever lay in store for us. After all, we had survived the period described in the Feb. 15, 1979 Herald thus: "Randolph thermometers registered lower than minus 40 degrees on Monday, while in some, the mercury disappeared altogether. The supreme universal desire, after four days when temperatures never got up near zero, was just to be warm."

**2002:**

*I sing a song of winter blues - long blue shadows stretched across the snow by early morning sun, and the deep blue of distant mountains, shouldering the burden of winter. The sky itself was less often blue than a colorless white, foretelling some form of inclement weather....*

*Of all the cold months of winter, February, providentially, has the fewest days - days which are lengthening and leading up to the unpredictable time of sugaring. Why, maple syrup has been made as early as the middle of the month.*

**February 15-21:**

*This 12 inch snowfall business was getting to be a habit. No sooner had we shoveled out from last weekend's heavy snows than another foot of the white stuff fell on Tuesday. All the next day the wind blew, piling up drifts, the like of which had not been seen for years. Schools were closed as men with snowplows battled the elements.*

*From then on, the sun dominated days, starting below zero and warming up moderately, and the waning crescent moon skimmed through chilly night skies.*

*It was a stark black and white world, beautiful in its clarity, that greeted us daily. Snowbanks mounted ever higher, as another five inches of snow fell Sunday night.*

*Most Vermont roofs are built with enough pitch to shed their burden of snow, but heavily laden flatter roofs require shoveling under present conditions. Did someone mention global warming?* 1993

February can produce its own bitter cold as well; from the third week of February, 1979:

*The trusty north-side thermometer on which this column depends did not register above zero for 230 hours, the period from Feb. 9 through noon, Feb. 18. Then after reaching one above, it dropped to 18 degrees below again.*

*Certainly this has been our trial by cold.*

*Continuous below-zero temperatures, coupled with daily winds from 20 to 30 mph, resulted in wind chill equivalents of nearly 70 degrees below zero at times.*

From the third week of February, 1982:

*Quiet, snow-covered hills, broken occasionally by the tracks of wild creatures, seem clothed in the soft brown fur of distant tree-tops. Nearer home, mounds of snow continue to mount higher, to the delight of small boys, while some driveways resemble snow tunnels.*

**1983:**

*Last Monday the snow fell purposefully all day, until a foot of the fluffy white stuff had accumulated, to be drifted higher by winds. It was a time for cat and dog to stretch out lazily indoors, aware of the raging elements.*

*Windblown white wraiths whirled from rooftops and along hard-packed snowy roads where a horse and sleigh would have felt at home on Tuesday.*

From 1988 on the value of a good snowstorm:

*Skiers were in seventh heaven and skaters glided across the ice joyfully. Sugarmakers felt that this year's maple crop would be better because of the deep snow. Householders recognized it as insulation and gardeners knew it as a source of nitrogen. It was a good storm after all!*

And from 1999 some real history:

*In 1781, the year our town was chartered, the corresponding week began with little snow, but within seven days it was 4-1/2 feet deep! This interesting information comes from Jonathan Carpenter's Journal[3], and he records several more storms of a foot or more, before declaring on April 26 it "looked melancholy to see snow on the level 2 feet deep." What happened once can always happen again.*

February 22-28:

*We started this year with less than 9 hours of daylight; now there are more than 11! But, according to the old saying,*

> *"As the days begin to lengthen,*
> *The cold begins to strengthen."*

*And so we shiver inside our citadels, besieged by the white army of winter. Now wild birds find many of their food sources covered in deep snow, so it is all the more important to keep seeds and suet available. Even oversized crows are daring to frequent local feeders.*

*The sharpness of hillsides of evergreens was softened by their snowy burdens, and most days were dazzling with sunshine. In the early evening, Venus and the nearby crescent moon made a picturesque sight.*

*Despite the frigid weather, thoughts were turning towards sugaring as town meeting day approached.* 1993

However consider this contrast from the fourth week of February, 1984:

*Bombarded by rain and sun's warm rays, snowmen grew to resemble dingy Venus de Milos, before collapsing on their knees in surrender. Trees carved out circles in the snow around them, then emerged on bare ground once more.*

*Mudtime, the bane of a mother's existence, but the joy of small fry, was here unexpectedly early, with all its oozy attraction. Pussywillow catkins swelled and green grass was actually visible in spots.*

*And while earthlings reveled in springtime thoughts and behavior, the full moon majestically swept through the dark skies above.*

And more thoughts on the coming of spring from 1985:

*Lengthening daylight hours gave signals to plants waiting under the snow that the growing season was approaching. And to gardeners with itchy fingers, the calendar would soon indicate indoor planting time for early flowers and vegetables.*

*At the end of the week the fingers of rain scrubbed away at the snow cover, which at no time had been deep (this winter).*

---

[3] *Jonathan Carpenter's Journal*, Edited by Miriam and Wes Herwig, 1994.

# March

THE MYSTERY OF VERMONT'S SWEET SUGARING SEASON AND THE STATE'S RENOWNED LEADERSHIP IN THE MAKING OF MAPLE SYRUP DOMINATE THE NATURAL NEWS OF THE MONTH OF MARCH. THERE IS NO GREATER INTERCONNECTION BETWEEN THE DAILY DETAILS OF WEATHER, COMMERCE AND NATURE THAN THE SUGARING SEASON, AND EACH YEAR FARMERS AND MAPLE SYRUP PRODUCERS TRACK TEMPERATURES AND SNOW COVER DAILY IN THE CONTINUING SEARCH FOR JUST THE RIGHT CONDITIONS FOR THE PRODUCTION OF THIS MOUTH-WATERING PRODUCT. THE COLUMNS AND EXCERPTS BELOW ILLUSTRATE THIS, AS WELL AS THE RATHER WIDE RANGE OF WEATHER CONDITIONS THAT CAN BOTH PLEASE AND FRUSTRATE SUGARING IN THE HEART OF VERMONT. AS WITH THE MONTH OF FEBRUARY PRECEDING, FOUR CONTINUOUS WEEKS FROM A SINGLE YEAR (1979) OF MIM'S COLUMNS PROVIDED THE BEST OVERALL VIEW OF THIS MOST CAPRICIOUS OF VERMONT'S WEATHER MONTHS, WHICH FEATURE EVERYTHING FROM SEVERE WIND AND BLIZZARDS TO EARLY SPRING CONDITIONS ACCOMPANIED BY PLENTY OF MUD.

March 1-7:

*In spring a young man's fancy lightly turns to thoughts of sugaring, in Vermont. Last week's above-freezing days and melting snowbanks are forerunners of that sweetest season of the year - sugaring.*

*There was not a cloud in the skies last Wednesday, as the warm sunshine melted snowbanks, forming little rivulets on hill roads and huge pools on level streets. The vision of such a beautiful day had sustained us during the rigors of winter, and now revived our winter-weary hearts.*

*Lengthening days alone are cause for rejoicing as we approach the vernal equinox. Sap has started surging up in the vast army of maple trees on our hillsides. Of course, it rises in all the native trees, but much experimenting has proven that no other produces a sweet syrup.*

*This is the season of expectancy, of snowmen and pussy-willows, blustering winds and beguiling sun. In short, Mother Nature is playing her prelude to spring.*    1979

March can come in roaring; from 1980:

*March came in like a lion, perhaps a stiff-jointed elderly lion whose cold breath chilled its prey, but a lion nevertheless. On three mornings last week the thermometer read 14 degrees below zero, which is also the lowest reading for the season...*

*(But) soon the miracle of spring will be enacted again, with the maple trees staging Scene One.*

Winter restarted, interrupting an early season maple sap run in March 1981:

*Last Wednesday's unexpected snow fall of ten inches, after many days of warm weather and bare ground, could be compared to 1. falling in love again or 2. going back to jail, depending on your outlook.... Temporarily stopped was the flow of maple sap, although good syrup had been made earlier than could be remembered before.*

1988:

*After two years with abominable sugaring weather, sugarmakers were on their mark, ready to go as soon as Mother Nature gave the signal. According to the University of Vermont, maple sugar contains calcium, potassium, magnesium, phosphorous, manganese and iron - all these plus a heavenly flavor!*

March 8-14:

*By Town Meeting Day, snow had settled dramatically, almost a foot in 24 hours, and it was a joy to see bare ground again, even if it did mean mud season was upon us. Tuesday's rain did not dampen our spirits, for it signaled time to plant tomatoes and start sugaring in earnest.*

*For three days the thawing weather continued, with sunshine and clouds alternating, and snow settling. But by the weekend winter had the land firmly in its grip again, with flurries of snow blown by 30 mph winds. Dirty snowbanks had a respectable covering of new snow, and sugarmakers were in a holding pattern as the temperature dipped to 10 degrees.*

1979

From the second week of March, 1980:

*Town meeting day brought typically encouraging weather with melting snow and thoughts of sugaring. By the end of the week, buckets and tubing were in place on maples, awaiting the first run of sap.*

*Distant hills are clothed with the soft brown fur of leafless trees. Relieving the subdued coloring of the landscape are occasional touches of red dogwood bushes and stretches of golden swamp grass rising above the scanty snow. This is a time of expectancy, when winter winds still vie with lengthening sunny days for possession of the land.*

1982:

*March stalked in like a stiff-legged lion, surveying the bleak scene with a cold eye. Temperatures dropped far below zero on three days last week, and the ever present wind hit 60 mph on Friday, tying a five-year record set last December.*

*Vermont character is supposed to be molded in part by endurance of our severe winters. If so, the current weather is doing some fine character-honing..... Snow is deeper than at any point this season, sometimes blocking the lower half of windows, giving a cave like atmosphere to darkened rooms.*[4]

1990:

*The brightest spot in last week's up and down weather was the discovery of white snowdrop buds bravely poking up through the snow Friday. On that same day maple sap surged upward as the age-old springtime ritual of tapping took place nearby. Once again there was the heady aroma of sap evaporating on the kitchen stove, and the sensation that life held better things in store.*

---

[4]Editor's note: The 1982 description matches well our conditions in early March 2005. As I work upon this book we're in the middle of an old fashioned blizzard, with 5 degree temperatures and heavy snow accompanied by 35 mph winds.

March 15-21:

*It must be confessed that this column is written on a mountaintop which has a monopoly on snow. Although it has settled considerably, white is still the predominant color hereabouts.*

*According to the calendar, spring begins this week, but seasoned inhabitants know that spring's arrival depends on the capriciousness of wind and sun. Winter claimed most of last week, with three zero mornings, and general wind velocity up to 30 mph.*

*On Wednesday, however, conditions were just right for sap to run and little boys to get muddy. This Monday proved to be the kind of day sugarmakers had been hoping for.* 1979

From the third week of March, 1981:

*No doubt about it - last week was, first and foremost, sugaring weather. The steady dripping of maple sap was music to the ears of sugarmakers, young and old. The rewarding sweet results seemed to gleam with the reds and golds of last fall's foliage, distilled. Cold nights and warming days provided the perfect conditions for good runs.*

*...At the time of the Great Blizzard of 1888, the Randolph newspaper described huge drifts which made traveling almost impossible and stopped trains. "The water system has stood the test of the severely cold weather perfectly," it stated. Ninety-three years later, the same system did not fare so well!*

Winter conditions resumed in mid-March accompanied by typical high-velocity Center winds in 1984:

*...Frigid, below-zero weather followed, climaxing Sunday with howling winds that tore over our hilltop like a freight train, at speeds over 60 miles per hour. In their wake, broken branches were scattered across the snow.*

*Our breath rose in plumes, as smoke spiraled from the chimneys of our snug homes. We were in a holding pattern; aware that it would be only a matter of time before the traditional forces of evil would be overcome by good.*

From mid-March, 1986:

*Sugaring started later than usual, but an entry from the journal of an ancestor in Dummerston [Vermont], who may have been the state's first white sugarmaker, read on March 19, 1764, "Tapped trees, made 21 pounds of molasses."*

More on the history of the Blizzard of 1888 from Mim's March 17, 1988 column:

*It was 100 years ago last week that the Blizzard of '88 buried the Northeast with an average of three feet of snow. Dr. Herbert Allen, whose dentistry some still remember, told that "you couldn't see a fence post between Randolph Center and North Randolph." According to Harry Cooley's history, it took twelve horses to pull the snow roller from Randolph to Bethel, houses were covered above the windows and paths became tunnels.*[5]

*Awesome as that blizzard was, even worse devastation was caused by the Great Snow of 1717. Although no white men inhabited Vermont that early, it was estimat-*

---

[5]*Randolph Vermont Historical Sketches*, by Harry H. Cooley; Edited by Miriam Herwig, 1978

*ed that 95% of the deer population, immobilized by the snow, was killed by wolves or bears.*

*By comparison, our week was mild. Sap ran, snow settled and mud oozed. Then on Thursday and Friday, howling winds caused chills of 30 degrees below zero. All in all, it was typical weather to expect of March.*

And on another blizzard, the big eastern snow storm of March, 1993:[6]

*As if on cue, celebrating the infamous Blizzard of 1888, the Blizzard of 1993 struck on the weekend...There were whiteouts and drifts of four feet or more, as road crews valiantly battled the elements all night.*

*Winds rose Sunday morning to higher velocities than they had for three years, buffeting houses while packing white insulation half way up windows. Not since late December 1962, when true blizzard conditions prevailed, have we experienced such severe weather. Old-timers can recall 8 - and 10 - foot drifts blocking all Center roads, and many motorists being stranded then. May this be winter's last and worst blow!*

March 22-28:

*The delightfully warm and sunny spring days last week seemed to come as a reward for enduring the rigors of winter. In contrast to the zero days of the week before, cloudless blue skies and balmy weather brought fresh hope to spirits locked too long in the jaws of winter.*

*Those massive mounds of plowed-back snow which looked as if they would last until June have shriveled into dirty heaps on the corners. Sturdy snow-drops are revealed in full bloom as the snow melts away.*

*Before our very eyes nature is staging the rejuvenation of earth, with flocks of early arrivals - redwings, cowbirds and grackles - turning up in the trees.*

*The weekend rain hastened the snow's disappearing act, and Monday's flurries did not amount to much.*                                                    1979

From the fourth week of March, 1981:

*...On Tuesday, the temperature dropped to zero, but no day was warm enough to coax sap out of temperamental maples. The first day of spring came and went, on the calendar, but not on the land.... At many lower elevations, the ground had appeared mostly bare, but Randolph Center had maintained its white covering, and its reputation for diehard winters.*

*In an average year, bluebirds, robins and song sparrows would have returned by now, but our ears are still expectantly listening for their songs. The longer Vermonters endure winter, the sweeter spring will seem to them.*[7]

---

[6]The editor will forever recall this storm since I was attending the wedding of a student friend in Pennsylvania, who endured leaks from the church roof and the loss of 95% of the guests who were unable to drive to the rural barn location for the reception. My wife and I ended up stranded in Pennsylvania for three additional days when the state closed most of its major highways.

[7]Editor's note: As I prepare this section in late March 2005 the words almost seem to fit perfectly, the ground has held its mantle of slightly graying white with no sign of robin or song sparrow. Mim called me a few days ago to exclaim how her snow drops had bloomed through the waning snow cover, an annual precursor to spring.

From late March, 1982:

*Last week we might have joined whole trees full of red-wings chortling their jubilation at the return of spring... Sap rose in maples as it has since time immemorial, and dripped into buckets to gladden the hearts of sugarmakers, big and small.*

*Velvety pussy willows ventured forth in the sunshine, and surely, under the snow, shoots of bulbs headed upward toward the light. Then on Sunday came an incongruous thunderstorm in the midst of falling snow. The old saying goes, "As many frosts in May as thunderstorms in March." We shall see.*

On another later winter snowstorm from 1984:

*Last week's big surprise was a snowstorm which dumped two feet of snow overnight, when only a few inches had been predicted. It may well be the deepest March snowfall in Vermont history for this area, since the famous Blizzard of '88 deposited only 20 inches in northern Vermont over a three-day period, concentrating on southern New England. And there were no Vermont inhabitants to record the only other rival, the Great Snow of 1717.*

Mim reported on a welcome variety of bird activity in late March, 1987:

*An assortment of newcomers had become established at local feeding grounds-cowbirds, grackles and redwings joining the ever present flocks of starlings, bluejays, mourning doves, red polls and evening grosbeaks. The early morning air was filled with bird-song which had been missing all winter. A most welcome sound was the liquid warble of bluebirds returning.*

On historical sugaring from late March 1988:

*Until a hundred years ago, the only way to store maple was to stir it into sugar and keep it in large wooden tubs. My grandmother told of feeling lucky to trade maple for white sugar, pound for pound.*

March 27 - April 2:

*March went out like a lamb, a wet, new-born one wrapped in a blanket of fog for two days. Last week's moisture-laden, dark days could best be described as dismal, with no rays of sunshine to brighten our outlook.*

*On Sunday patches of snow were scattered here and there like isolated enemy forces surrendering to the conquering army of spring. It was a temporary victory, however, for on Monday April capriciously covered us with white again.*

*Sap has run by fits and starts with an earlier-than-usual end of sugaring predicted. Monday's snow was good for saving to store in the freezer for future sugar-on-snow parties, as well as for snowballs.*                              1979

March to April, 1981:

*"For lo, the winter is past... the time of the singing of birds is come," says the Song of Solomon. Whole trees full of returning redwings and their relatives fill the air with joyful, if somewhat unmelodic, paeans to spring.*

*Hardy little snowdrops, set out by the early settlers, show their white blooms, and velvety pussy willows reach toward the blue sky.*

*Despite mainly warming temperatures, sugaring continued unabated throughout last week. Sugar snow fell on Friday, but was not long for this world, as all accumulated snow did a disappearing act in the heavenly warmth of the weekend.*

*Only strong winds on Sunday marred the warmest day of the year. But mud underfoot could not dampen spirits released from the long, cold burden of winter.*

From the end of March, 1982:

*Last week specialized in sugar weather, when yesterday's mud freezes hard and yesterday's puddles turn to splintery ice in the morning, while robins cheerily announce their home-coming.*

*Trees were encircled by rings of bare ground and snow on the level was only knee deep, half what it had been a week earlier. But Old Man Winter does not give up easily, and on the weekend he let loose with buffeting 55 mph winds and zero temperatures, which set back the calendar considerably.*

Some weather lore from Mim's column in late March, 1983:

*It seems that we are bound to get our quota of winter weather sooner or later, and March is preferable to April-or May-for frigid conditions. Perhaps the old saying, "Better to see the devil than a robin in March" had some foundation in fact!*

From 1984:

*...In such warm, inviting weather, mud was accepted as a necessary evil. The sound of eaves dripping was music to our ears. Snow shriveled under the sun's rays like puckered white leather.*

*The first adventurous robin made his appearance, likewise the first audacious skunk!*

On the lateness of the onset of the sugaring season in 1989:

*"Wednesday (the 22nd) was not sugaring weather either, but - praise be - sap ran well on Thursday. About time, although some can remember that the 1949 season was even later."*[8]

---

[8]Editor's note: We did not begin boiling in the Center in 2005 until the same time.

# April

WE ARE ALL FAMILIAR WITH THE SAYING "APRIL SHOWERS BRING MAY FLOWERS." WE HAVE OUR SHARE OF APRIL SHOWERS IN CENTRAL VERMONT, BUT SEVERAL OF THEM ARE OFTEN FROZEN INSTEAD OF LIQUID IN NATURE. THESE BACK AND FORTH SHOWERS ARE EMBLEMATIC OF THE CONTINUING TUSSLE BETWEEN THE ONSET OF SPRING AND THE RECURRING BOUTS OF "OLD MAN WINTER." THE SNOW EVENTUALLY RECEDES LEAVING MUD SEASON; WE DON OUR BOOTS IN EXPECTATION THAT THE GREENING OF SPRING IS UPON US. SUGARING SEASON WANES AS SNOW DISAPPEARS. ENJOY MIM'S COLUMNS ABOUT THE FIRST FLOWERING BULBS, THE ACTIVITY OF THE BIRDS AND THE CONQUEST OF SPRING.

April 2 - 8:

*As Mark Twain said a hundred years ago, there is a sumptuous variety about New England weather that compels the stranger's admiration and regret.*

*This past week has been one for regret, with snow and winds producing highway reports of awful traveling on Saturday. Snowplows were out combating the winter weather. Wind chill equivalents reached minus 20° at times, while a blanket of snow protected bulbs which had shot up in the previous warmth.*

*Sunday's sunshine was welcome, nurturing hopes for a second arrival of spring and a speedy thawing of the white covering surrounding us. These hopes were dashed Monday by another snowstorm and accompanying gusts of wind. For such times our ancestors must have coined the maxim, "What can't be cured must be endured." 1979*

From the same week in 1984:

*"Slow but steady wins the race," as the hare said, and it is true we have made progress since a week ago. The patches of snow are diminishing and the mud is beginning to dry up. Sugaring is on its last legs as the frog run approaches.*

Waiting for spring during a wintry first week of April, 1985:

*Last Monday started with an April Fool joke - snow-covered ground which had been bare when darkness fell the night before. But this snow was not just a passing thing - each day added more inches to our winter-white blanket.*

*True, it was perfect for sugar-on-snow and for snowmen, but our minds had become attuned to such spring-like matters as crocus blooms and fresh-dug parsnips.*

*It was waiting weather... waiting for the warm sun to shine again and a tinge of green to appear on drab lawns.*

From the first week of April, 1990:

*The Vermont version of walking on water - crunching around on the snow crust - occurred last Monday, recalling many exciting sliding episodes. A spring phenomenon was noticeable at the bird feeder - the ivory beaks of evening grosbeaks were turning green!*

From 1994:

*The business of the day was sugaring last week, as sap rose in the trees, and hope rose in our hearts. Mud was a sure sign of the season, but so were the returning birds - redwings, grackles, cowbirds, song sparrows, robins and bluebirds.*

April 9 - 15:

*The early arrival of spring, without setbacks so far, is almost too good to be true. Delicate hepaticas and spring beauties bloom on wooded hillsides, while nearer home daffodils and tulips push high, and lawns bring thoughts of mowing once more.*

*It has not always been thus. Only two years ago [see excerpt from1979 following], the comparable week contained four snowy days and blustery winter weather. Early Randolph settler Jonathan Carpenter wrote in his diary on April 18, 1781, that snow was a foot deep on the level and pond ice had not "broke up."*

*But, on waking, we can revel in the soft greens of nature instead of the long-familiar glare of snow. Each in his own way is grateful for this season of rebirth.* 1981

But see the same weekly period from 1979:

*At this elevation, 1384 feet above sea level, there was snow on the ground all week, dazzling in Wednesday's sunshine, and gleaming in the light of the full moon. On Thursday and Friday the temperature climbed nicely, but the wind was from the East, an ill omen. And on Saturday snow fell all day, a discouraging sight for Easter weekend.*

*Fog heralded Easter morning, and skies were overcast all day, not the time for spring finery yet. A few bright crocuses, blue scillas and pastel hyacinths poked their buds through the snow, but green-up is still to come. By nightfall a drizzle was pecking away at the snow remaining on the ground.*

*However, falling snow greeted everyone Monday morning, with a substantial covering on the ground. It used to be referred to as "the poor man's manure," for spring snow combines more nitrogen than spring rain, and grass springs up green after it melts.*

And worse yet, just one year removed from the idyllic spring conditions described in 1981, read the summary from the second week of April, 1982:

*Winter had saved its worst blizzard for last, we discovered last week to our sorrow. On Wednesday wicked winds thundered by like express trains as much as 67 mph, breaking the 7-year records at the Center. New snow drifted in places and in others the earth was swept bare. Combined with zero temperatures, the results were wind chills of 50° below!*

*It was a cruel greeting for newly returned spring birds, and hard enough for sturdy natives to face. But gradually winter released its icy grip, till Easter Sunday was blessed with sunshine and warmth. Living with Vermont weather can be compared to getting married - it's for better, for worse!*

Yet see the hope expressed in 1986:

*It seems that we must endure our quota of winter, whether all in one piece, or interspersed with unseasonably warm days... All in good time would come the weather we were longing for - the biblical time of the singing of birds - also the plowing of gardens and blooming of daffodils.*

Mim comments on the end of the sugaring season from the second week of April, 1992:

*Browns were the shades of earth last week- the chocolate color of mud, the rose beige of matted dry leaves and the tan of winter-weary lawns....*

*And through all spring's vicissitudes, maple sugaring continued by fits and starts, in this banner year. Not even the wisest prognosticator could have predicted such a bountiful yield, proving again how mysterious weather is.*

A year when mid-April was peak mud season; 1993:

*Last Monday's landscape resembled a brown-and-white spotted puppy, with more brown hourly, as cold rain pelted down. Tuesday was a gray day, but Wednesday, praise be, was sunny and warmer.*

*Earth was at its lowest point - soggy, dark and desolate in the last stages of pregnancy- but the promise of tender green life was in the air. A few blades of grass daringly appeared, and purple crocuses opened, a full week late.*

April 16-23:

*Last Monday was nice, but Tuesday was nicer. In fact, it was glorious! Sunday's two inch snowfall had vanished. Growth, which had been at a standstill, was coaxed upward by the sun. Wednesday's drizzle and Friday's rain brought fresh green tones to bedraggled lawns, and dandelion greens began appearing.*

*It is not until we experience the warmth and freedom of spring days that we realize what a social barrier winter has been. Neighbors, who have been separated by snow and cold, emerge from winter quarters into the bright sunshine with hearty greetings.*

*Winds were bone-chilling on Sunday, which felt more like March than April. Nevertheless, birds were returning according to schedule, with tree swallows gracefully swooping over the water, and flickers drumming. The sweet, shrill chorus of peepers announced that spring was really here.*[9]                    1995

From the third week of April, 1979:

*Spring coyly retreated and advanced the past week, scattering showers here and there, with strong winds counteracting the sun's warmth to some extent. Then came Saturday, the most glorious day of the year so far. The sun beamed down, driving householders out to tackle winter's cleanup with enthusiasm. Whatever the task, there was joy in just being alive...*

---

[9]Editor's note: My son, Geoffrey and I track the first peepers annually and as I continue work on this book in mid-April 2005, we have just returned from an outdoor expedition here in the Center aimed at hearing and seeing the sounds of the new season. It is always music to the ears after another long winter.

More beautiful spring weather from 1980:

*Saturday brought the beautiful sunshine we had been waiting for, when humans emerged from winter chrysalises in the inviting warmth. Lawn raking was actually tempting, and there was one last belated run of sap.*

From the third week of April, 1986:

*Although banks of snow on the north side of buildings and in the deep woods stubbornly resisted the advance of spring, the forces of warmth were surely winning.*

*Mourning doves cooed plaintively in the early hours of the day, and swamp maple buds displayed the redness that foretold their autumn splendor.*

*Jaded appetites were tempted by dandelion and cowslip greens, as well as fresh-caught trout. The smell of newly turned loam lured long-dormant gardeners, and nest-building was the main order of business for early birds.*

The coming of spring flowers in 1987:

*The gold of daffodils brightened our dwellings, and out in the woods hepaticas, wild ginger, spring beauty and adder tongues opened their dainty blooms. It was a time of rejoicing.*

From 1994:

*Catkins hung from poplar trees in anticipation of fairer days ahead, and daffodils budded... Wakeup songs of robins sounded in early mornings, replacing the chill silence of winter. Red buds were swelling on swamp maples, an echo of their flaming fall beauty, and dandelion greens were sprouting. Perhaps we had seen the last of snow for another six months!*[10]

April 24-30:

*The last vestige of snow disappeared from the premises with April's passing, and a hundred shades of green were a sight for sore eyes. Robins sounded their wakeup calls by 5 a.m. as daylight hours continued to expand. Ferns uncurled their shepherds' crooks and dandelion greens provided a spring tonic for winter-jaded appetites.*

*Jaunty tulips and daffodils burst into bloom as days grew warmer and sunnier. True, Monday's temperatures had dropped and cold rain had fallen. But after that, the weather had improved steadily.*

*The hardships of last winter faded like a bad dream in the balmy springtime atmosphere. Now wonders of nature were unfolding daily, and housebound spirits had the opportunity to rejoice with Browning - "God's in His heaven, all's right with the world!"*                                                                          1993

From the last week of April, 1980:

*The surest sign that spring is here to stay is not a visible one at all. The serenade of choruses of peepers [in the] evenings is a signal that every small swamp and pond has warmed up enough to leave the fear of returning winter behind.*

---

[10]Editor's note: Mim called this one almost precisely! There were flurries once more in early May, followed by 6 months without snow before flurries flew in early November.

When daylight savings hours returned the last Sunday in April, 1985:

*Day after day, more delicate hues of green spread over the land, transforming its barrenness into a scene of restful beauty. Beds of sky-blue scillas bloomed as crocus faded, while in the woods spring beauty and hepaticas appeared.*

*The sun beamed down and winds blew, and suddenly a multitude of tasks confronted homeowners. The accumulation of winter's ravages demanded immediate attention.*

*With the sun, and little children, rising at an ever-earlier hour, the change to Daylight Savings was hailed as a blessing.*

On the last of the snow from late April, 1988:

*The last lingering pile of snow in the village, suspiciously near our thermometer, dwindled last Wednesday, after two days of sunshine and comparative warmth. Buds were actually swelling on the trees, making a delicate tracery against the sky.*

And from 1989, as spring gradually replaced the relics of winter:

*April resolutely held out until the end without raising false hopes of balmy weather. Buds were swelling on maple trees, and always there was the wind which is the Center's trademark. Kites dangling in treetops gave mute testimony to its capriciousness.*

*Gradual greening in certain spots and faint pink tones on the hillsides hinted at coming splendor. Along the interstate,[11] weeping willows glowed like giant golden bouquets.*

April concludes with something from the history books, transcribed by Mim in 1994:

*...piles of snow shrank but did not disappear. Lest we feel that spring has been long in coming, read about what happened here 120 years ago:*

*On April 30, 1874, a foot of snow fell on top of a 15 inch snowfall on the 26th, making a grand total of 49 inches for the month of April.*

*Compare that with the total snowfall for the winter of 1912-13 of only 31 inches, and it is very evident why weather prediction in Vermont is such a challenge.*

---

[11]Route # 89, from Concord, New Hampshire to the Vermont-Canadian border at Highgate

# May

OLD MAN WINTER HAS USUALLY GASPED HIS LAST BY EARLY MAY, THE MONTH THAT SPRING ACTUALLY BREAKS OUT IN THE GREEN MOUNTAIN STATE. EVER SO GRADUALLY THE TREES DISPLAY A SPECIAL PASTEL GREEN THAT CREEPS UP THE MOUNTAINSIDES. FOREST FLOWERS, PERENNIALS AND TREES AND BUSHES BEGIN TO BLOOM. OF COURSE, WILDLIFE, ESPECIALLY THE BIRDS, ARE EXTREMELY ACTIVE AS THEY MOVE IN, MATE AND RAISE FAMILIES. THESE COLUMNS CAPTURE THE BEAUTY OF NATURE'S REBIRTH, SO EVIDENT DURING THIS SPECIAL MONTH.[12]

May 1-7:

*Though some days last week were discouraging, dropping to the freezing mark, just compare with last year. Then snow fell on May first and temperatures started out in the twenties for four days, so we're really ahead of the game.*

*Wind has averaged more than 20 mph every day, drying out the land for planting. Dandelion and cowslip greens have been plentiful, as have been worms for fishing. There has been no sudden surge of growth in days that have been mainly chilly, but slow and steady wins the race.*

*Maple leaves are the size of a mouse's ear, an indication on old-time seed packets that seeds could be safely planted in the warming soil. This is such a busy time of year that picturesque cumulus clouds floating in the blue sky may go entirely unnoticed.*

1979

Descriptive words from the onset of May in 1980:

*Buckeyes are opening green leafy fingers to the sky, swamp maples are decorated with red lace and poplars and willows dot the landscape with their bright yellow-greens. Forsythias, which usually bloom well only below the snow line because of our severe winters, are putting on a special golden glow.*

From the first week of May, 1981:

*These days bring unexpected joys - a lawn carpeted with pale blue violets, shadbush in dainty white bloom or a robin's nest perched atop a pick-axe in a shed...*

*Sunshine coaxed soft tones of green from wooded hillsides and made mundane chores seem enticing. Kites soared on high and ball games sprang up as naturally as grass.*

A paragraph from early May, 1992:

It was a time of newness and rebirth, when the fetters of bleak winter were released, and spirits expanded along with leaf buds. Robins patiently brooded their eggs, while humans with great expectations planted gardens.

---

[12]Editor's note: There were so many beautiful descriptions to draw upon this month that I was unable to limit my selections to less than four per week and for the mid-month period opted to include two different full-length examples from different years.

The swift pace of change in early May was expressed by Mim in 2000:

*Fiddleheads shot up into tall ferns in a matter of days, while leaves were expanding right and left. More growth and change were packed into these seven days than at any other such period all year. It was a heady sensation to be in the midst of this rapid transformation of our world, to be swept up by a host of seasonal demands.*

A look back at May history, which sometimes included late bouts with "Old Man Winter," from the first May column in 1994:

*Gradually our eyes adjusted to the soft tones of the earth, mainly browns and greens, instead of the bleak whiteness which we had long endured. True, there were flurries in the air Monday, but no lasting accumulation.*

*There are those who remember the late snowfalls of 1967, when six inches fell on May 8th and another six inches May 25, and thank our lucky stars that such weather has not been repeated.*

May 8 - 14:

*Spring was making up for lost time by leaps and bounds last week. At first there were puffs of shad blossoms along the roadsides, and then, amazingly, apple trees burst into fragrant bloom. The wind brought a new sound not heard for six months - the rustling of a million leaves. And those leaves began providing dappled shade on every side.*

*Latecomers in the bird world - saucy catbirds, rollicking bobolinks, brilliant orioles and diminutive hummingbirds - were all staking out their territories.*

*Tuesday's temperature was the highest this year, and not surprisingly, a brief thunderstorm rumbled through. Quite the opposite was true Friday morning when there was frost nearby.*

*This most beautiful season was rushing by far too fast, with a myriad of pressing duties keeping our noses to the grindstone, so to speak. However, colder weather on Sunday held some of the rainbow flowers in check. But no rose was ever without a thorn - pesky black flies were threatening the quality of outdoor living!*       1993

From the second week of May, 1982:

*After a week of sunshine and dappled shade, last Saturday was perfect for graduating, gardening or going fishing. Baltimore orioles and bobolinks, late-comers from the South, reclaimed the blue skies with their joyous singing.*

*The growth on our cold mountain-top is later than in surrounding valleys, for here dandelion fields have not yet turned gold, and locust trees stand bare, still reluctant to leaf out.*

Winter's last gasp from mid-May 1983:

*As late-arriving hummingbirds darted among daffodils, it was easy to forget the winter conditions of a few days earlier. On Monday cold rain had turned to snow, and on Tuesday morning the ground was white in grassy places. Hail fell at noon, and Wednesday was still cold and rainy....Yet [by week's end] Saturday's sunny warmth compensated for all deprivations - the world was beautiful again.*

Here is a depiction of environmental change within our lifetimes; in this case the loss of the stately elm trees mentioned in May, 1986:

*Baltimore orioles came back on their appointed date Saturday [the 10th], finding fewer and fewer of their favorite nesting trees, elms.*[13]

On the magic of spring, 1989:

*Gentle midweek rains spurred the grass to new heights, while the smell of fresh-turned earth gladdened the hearts of gardeners everywhere. Orioles sang from tree-tops, sporting the colors of Lord Baltimore - orange and black. If time could be caught in a bottle, the coming May days would surely be the ones to preserve, when spirits are lifted by the warmth and sheer beauty of another returning spring.*

On the rapid transition of spring to early summer weather from May, 1998:

*"When lilacs last in the dooryard bloomed,"*[14] *it was after Memorial Day, the traditional time for their blossoming. Ever since the Civil War, their flowers have been used to decorate soldiers' graves.*

*But this year lilacs were extremely early in blooming, along with fragrant apple trees. Such beauty was welcomed with open arms, but accompanied by a twinge of concern, for the latest date to expect frost in this neck of the woods is June 9! The season was on fast forward, with hot, summery days in sharp contrast to the cool, rainy weather of the week before.*

Mim commented upon the progression of different tree species in 2002:

*Tree silhouettes separated the progressives from the conservatives last week. Locusts stood austerely bare and leafless, not daring to expose any foliage to the elements yet, while maples blithely opened their green umbrellas wider every day. Ash trees took the middle ground, testing the waters with their toes, so to speak.*

May 15-21:

*Last week was full of dandelion days, as cheerful golden patches covered fields and lawns. Hillsides wore a multitude of fresh tints, from light yellow and rose beige to tender greens as tree leaves unfurled.*

*Here and there were drifts of pale bluets, like late-fallen snow. It was not a year for forsythia, as 1987 had been, for last winter's deep freeze killed all flower buds except those beneath a shallow covering of snow, at this elevation.*

*A roof-shaking thunderstorm Monday night was followed by a week of damp, drizzly weather and fog that defied lawn mowing efforts. There were few glimpses of the sun, but growth spurted ahead just the same - ferns shot up and field grass was suddenly knee deep.*

---

[13]Editor's note: I asked Mim on a local history trip in the spring of 2005 about these birds and she said they have adapted for the most part to other trees including the maple. Unfortunately even our maples in the Center have shown much stress of late, which may be due to climate change or other environmental or soil condition factors.

[14]Walt Whitman

*The loveliest time of year was at hand, full of fragrance and color, but it was also a time of great activity. Harried bird parents flew back and forth to their nests, while beneath, humans plowed and planted.*  1988

*Everyone's favorite color at this time of year has to be green, visible in dozens of different hues, each restful to the eye. Catkins were dangling from birch trees and maples were fringed with yellowish-green flowers.*

*Delicate white puffs on the landscape indicated blossoming shadbush, which was so named by early settlers when the shad [fish] run upstream occurred.*

*The return of the last of our migrant birds, even though a wee bit late, brought a sense of satisfaction, as treetops, bushes and air itself were filled with activity and song. Indigo buntings, rose-breasted grosbeaks and yellow warblers were highlights among the foliage, and hummingbirds caused joy all out of proportion to their size.*

*Young and old alike were seized with the age-old urge to be part of the miracle of growth through gardening. Two of the delights of spring were homegrown - the first meals of asparagus and rhubarb.*

*Vast armies of dandelions held fields and lawns under their golden sway. Earth was at its loveliest.*  1995

From 1979:

*The fragrance of apple blossoms and lilacs drifts through the air, providing an ideal background for graduations and weddings. Dandelions' gold glorifies lawns and fields, and rhubarb patches yield juicy pies.*

*Spring seems to be rushing headlong into summer, without giving anyone time to fully enjoy it. It is hard to tell which grows faster - the grass which needs to be mowed or the weeds which need to be pulled.*

Mim quotes from Jonathan Carpenter's diary in 1980:

*Two hundred years ago, when central Vermont towns were beginning to be settled, Jonathan Carpenter, one of Randolph's earliest residents, kept a diary. On May 19 he recorded:*

*"Fryday, remarkable dark about 12 o'clock, but no rain."*

*This phenomenon was later ascribed to forest fires far to the west in New York State, and was not a solar eclipse.*

This is the best time of year for Mim as expressed in 1981 and again in 1985:

*If the clock could be stopped at any one point, this would be the time to do it, with all the tender loveliness of spring bursting forth. But seasons move relentlessly on, and each day must be enjoyed to the fullest.*

*Last week, maple trees were fringed with yellow-green florets and birches scattered their caterpillar-like catkins. Fragile blue eggshells turned up on the grass and returning orioles sang exuberantly from the treetops.*

*There can be no lovelier time than mid-May in Vermont, with barn swallows swooping about in the blue sky and delicate hues covering the hillsides. Yellow-green poplars, olive-green maples, rosy brown shrubs mingle fleetingly with multi-colored flowers. All too soon the deep greens of summer will predominate.*

Cold weather kept in our face in 1984 with snow flurries and hail the third week of May. This setback had Mim consulting historical records documenting weather here in the Center:

*Our recent persistent snow flurries and hail were discouraging, but there are those who remember the six-inch snowstorm at the end of the war in Europe on May 10, 1945... The Hibbard family of Randolph Center, which had kept weather records since 1870, did report an 18-inch snowfall on May 20, 1892. Of course, the greatest spring snow in Vermont history occurred in June 1816, drifting up to 20 inches toward the north.*

And more history quoted from Carpenter's journal about a cold May - June period from Mim's entry, after a very rainy and chilly third week of May, 1990:

*Lest anyone think 1990 is the pits, read what it was like 210 years ago, from the diary of Randolph pioneer, Jonathan Carpenter:*

*May 1, 1780 Very stormy, rain and snow*
*May ye 2nd snow ½ leg deep*
*May ye 6 snow and ice plenty*
*May ye 8 snow knee deep in some places*
*May ye 11 some snow*
*June 4th and 5th great frost*
*June 11th pretty cold for ye season - in grinding, water froze on ye grindstone*
*June ye 19th very cold for ye season*
*July 15th cold nights, some frost in low land*
*July ye 24th It now begins to be warm weather, the first we have had this summer.*[15]

When nature was at her peak of beauty, Mim reminded us of our duty to respect the landscape (1999):

*It was the most fragrant time of year, when apple blossoms and lilacs scented the air, and brilliantly colored orioles sang their rich melodies from tree tops... Vermont's hillsides were never greener, and it was our responsibility to cultivate and protect them so the generations to come might be able to enjoy them as we do.*

May 22 - 28:

*"Now if ever come perfect days," wrote Lowell about June, but it didn't seem days could get any more perfect than they were last Monday and Tuesday. After the monochromatic tedium of winter, the vibrant colors, evocative fragrances and musical sounds of spring all were balm to our spirits.*

*The bubbling songs of bobolinks floated over fields, and chimney swifts chittered high in the sky, while underfoot wild strawberry blossoms carpeted many lawns.*

*Apple trees were starting to bloom at this elevation, but lilacs had not yet opened, waiting for more warmth to turn them on.*

*Gardeners labored happily in vegetable plots and flower beds, although everyone commented on how dry it was. The whole year so far has had below-average precipitation.*

---

[15]Editor's note: This was not even 1816, otherwise known as 1800 and froze to death.

*Under clear blue skies, the hills of home never looked more beautiful, as flags rippled in the breeze and heads bowed in memoriam.*                                        1995

From the last week in May 1985:

*Century-old lilacs, redolent of Memorial Days past, were never lovelier than last Monday. Forget-me-nots, too, were reminders that, to live in hearts we leave behind is not to die.*

*Candle-like blossoms covered buckeye and horse chestnut trees, providing a paradise for humming birds. Rhubarb patches, which early settlers called pieplant, were in their prime, and lawns were visions of green velvet.*

*As the summer solstice approached, late shadows slanted across the hills from the northwest, marking days rich in contentment.*

A snapshot from late May, 1989:

*Pale gold candelabra-like blooms decorated buckeye trees. Almost in the wink of an eye, flowering crab trees became heavenly pink puffs, while the fragrance of apple blossoms was wafted on the breeze. And in another wink, it seemed, they were going by. Birdsong, which had filled the air from dawn to dusk was heard less frequently, as the young lovers had become parents working 15-hour days to feed their broods. Such is life!*

There are a few less pleasant occurrences at this time of year and Mim noted one in 1992:

*A forgotten benefit of winter is the absence of insects, which abound now in various shapes and sizes. June bugs bump against screens, earthworms do pushups, black flies and mosquitoes zoom in for a bite.*

May 29 - June 4:

*Memorial Day was laden with the fragrance of lilacs, the flower of remembrance. Lovingly planted by early settlers, the bushes nearby have bloomed for 175 years.*

*Tuesday took us by surprise, with haze and humidity. Fortunately, constant breezes seemed to drive pesky black flies into hiding. Rain began that night and continued off and on for two days. Then the threat of frost hung over us and the warm kitchen stove felt good. Such cool weather slowed down eager gardeners, who had to content themselves with juicy rhubarb pies and tender asparagus.*

*Seemingly as compensation for our trials and tribulations, the weekend turned out to be just what we'd been hoping for - sunny and warmer.*

*Swaths of new cut hay striped the fields, and candles of buckeye blossoms decorated tall trees. The green, green world was a delight to the eyes, and a challenge to the lawn mowers. "Summer is icumen in" as it did seven centuries ago.*[16]                    1994

More from late May, 1980 on my favorite flowering bush, the lilac:

*The nostalgic fragrance of lilacs is wafted on the breezes, bringing memories of servicemen, of loved ones gone, even of cellar holes guarded by lilac bushes. In New England, Memorial Day and lilacs are inseparable. Yet lilacs are believed to have originated in Persia and traveled to Europe via Constantinople and Vienna before the Mayflower sailed.*

---

[16]Geoffrey Chaucer

From late May into early June, 2001, on the spread of chervil and the promise of approaching summer:

*Spreading like wildfire across the countryside, dainty, white-flowered chervil has gone rampant along roadsides and every other place possible. Like the insidious kudzu of the south, this carrot-like weed is crowding out native plants and spreading into fields. Dried chervil has been used sparingly as an herb, but what a salvation it would be if some scientist, like George Washington Carver, should discover a major use for the ubiquitous chervil!...*

*Summer thunder growled around harmlessly like a bear with a full stomach. Summer must be just around the corner, we reasoned. Spring had been like babyhood, sweet and fleeting.*

Finally to close out this five week review from the month of May, here is a column Mim wrote after a particularly nasty Memorial Day weekend in 1997:

*When Was the Weather Worse?*

*So you think this Memorial Day weekend was the pits - that such foul weather has never before disgraced the fair state of Vermont!*

*Why, a mere 30 years ago, six inches of snow prevented Randolph Center school children from marching into the adjacent cemetery to lay flowers on the graves of soldiers on Memorial Day.*

*The range and unpredictability of Vermont weather demand a healthy respect. There have been May heat waves (1911 and 1964) as well as snowstorms (two feet on May 20, 1892, making six inches on Memorial Day 1967, look fairly mild). Eleven years ago, lilacs and apple blossoms had gone by, and the first crop of hay had been harvested by that same holiday. Then 1991 brought us the hottest May on record.*

*Have we forgotten that three to six inches of snow fell last year (at this time) in Lincoln? Local hills were spared such indignity, but, as history proves, it could always be worse, or better. This year, at least the only snow reported last week, six inches, was on the summit of Mt. Mansfield.*

*Philosophical Vermonters may grumble, but deep down, they know that our climate can't be beat!*

Geoffrey Doering

# June

THE HALCYON DAYS OF JUNE, THOSE PERFECTLY BLENDED DAYS OF BLUE SKIES, BRIGHT SUN-
SHINE, LONG DAYLIGHT HOURS AND GREEN GROWTH UNPARALLELED. LET ME QUOTE THE WRITING
OF JAMES RUSSELL LOWELL:

> "OH, WHAT IS SO RARE AS A DAY IN JUNE?
> THEN, IF EVER, COME PERFECT DAYS.
> WHEN HEAVEN TRIES EARTH IF IT BE IN TUNE
> AND OVER IT SOFTLY HER WARM EAR LAYS.
> WHETHER WE LOOK OR WHETHER WE LISTEN,
> WE HEAR LIFE MURMUR AND SEE IT GLISTEN."

June 4-10:

*Last week it seemed that every day was nicer than the one before, until Friday we could echo with James Russell Lowell, "Oh what it so rare as a day in June? Then, if ever, come perfect days."*

*Skies were blue and the sun kept getting warmer. This was the weather we had dreamed of through snow and freezing rain all winter, and there were no complaints, not one.*

*Days were at their longest - fifteen and a quarter hours of daylight - compared to nine at Christmas time. And those hours were filled with a multitude of activities - weeding and mowing, picnicking and hiking, to name a few.*

*One of the joys of the season was eating fresh asparagus. However, milkweed greens were not to be forgotten, and their flower buds, like broccoli, are loaded with vitamin C.*

*The weather in June, like any other time in Vermont, can be quirky. Take the same week in 1780 from Jonathan Carpenter's Journal, when he wrote, "pretty cold for ye season-great frost-ye water froze on ye grindstone in grinding," illustrating it with a picture of icicles on his fingers!*                                                          2001

From the first week of June, 1982:

*The dark green of summer foliage has replaced the tender hues of early spring....*

*Lest there be complaints about the weather, let it be remembered that not only was there a snowstorm June 7, 1816, but also a snowfall of one foot on June 11, 1842. Anything can happen in Vermont weather-and frequently does.*

From early June, 1986:

*Leafless locust trees, which had held out, stark and forbidding, finally broke forth in greenery last week. Along the roadsides there were lacy blossoms of thornapples and showy white fake flowers to lure pollinators to the hobble bush. It was early to see young robins with their spotted breasts venturing forth...*

*The first crop of hay on several local farms was harvested before June first - a record that may stand for many years. In an extreme comparison, the diary of Randolph's early settler, Jonathan Carpenter, tells of beginning to mow (by hand) on July 17 and finishing haying July 31, 1780 [nearby] in Pomfret. That year there was a frost July 15 and the first warm weather of the summer began July 24.*[17]

Before the crowding of the invasive chervil we had wild carrot blossoms, from 1988:

*Lacy wild carrot blossoms crowded the highways like extravagant ruffles, and dandelions, which had gilded fields so recently, were transformed into vagabond graybeards....*

*The age-old sweetness of new-mown hay rose again as farmers on tractors laid low the tall grass which our ancestors used to cut with swinging scythes.*

A perfect early June week described in 1997 when every day was sunny with temperatures in the 70s:

*Ladies and gentlemen, may I present one solid week of perfect weather!*

*Such blissful conditions, coming on the heels of May's abominable weather, were almost too good to be true.*

*Flowering pink crabs were visions of loveliness, and the air was redolent of apple blossoms. Asparagus and milkweed greens provided tasty eating...*

June 10- 16:

*Although last week began cool and rainy, perfect summer weather, visions of which had buoyed us through long winter days, was here at last. The freedom of stepping outdoors without wraps, of sleeping with windows open to fresh air, of waking to sunlight streaming in - all these were our constant blessings.*

*But for everything worthwhile there is a price to pay. For such Eden-like conditions, there was a horde of insects - buzzing, crawling, flying, stinging!*

*Across our hills, dainty thornapples were in bloom, and powder puff-laden dogwoods beautified roadsides. But there was one conspicuous absence at this elevation. Black locusts, whose sweet pea-like blossoms are usually perfuming the air at this time, had none this year, undoubtedly the result of a spring frost.*

*The hot humid weekend made the old swimming hole a popular place, but cool brick houses were a close second.* 1995

From 1987:

*Sunday was perfectly delightful, fitting Lowell's famous query, "And what is so rare as a day in June?" Locust trees, which a short time ago had been rugged, ungainly skeletons, were suddenly transformed with beautiful, fragrant panicles of sweetpea-like blossoms. These largest legumes on earth were brought here by early settlers, perhaps as much for their honey-making potential as their enduring quality as fence posts.*

*The sweetness of peonies and iris, and, yes, the smell of new-mown hay, would forever mingle with memories of graduation and end-of-school days.*

---

[17]Editor's note: Although this early June 1980 column has been lost to history, Mim indicates information worth noting - in sharp contrast to the warming conditions usually occurring at this time, she recorded four days of frost which covered gardens and even left some ice in her bird bath!

An early season heat wave described in 1988, which turned out to be a very warm summer:

*From near-freezing mornings the week before, our temperatures sky-rocketed to the 90's last Monday, Tuesday and Wednesday. Hardly a drop of rain had fallen in June; gardens and lawns were parched.*

*Cries of killdeer and chittering of chimney swifts sounded early in the day, but by noon a hot stillness prevailed. Shades were drawn and fans were running as record-breaking heat gripped the land.*

June 17-23:

*In the still, hot afternoons last week, birdsong ceased, except for the worry calls of parent robins or the twittering of chimney swifts high in the air. This was always a time of celebration of primitive peoples, when daylight peaked, the sun was warm and earth was fruitful.*

*Sweet, little wild strawberries ripened by the thousands in pastures, swamps and cemeteries, and gardens grew by leaps and bounds. The only rain that fell all week produced a beautiful triple rainbow Tuesday evening.*

*School was out and swimming became the order of the day. In the leafy shade and cooling breezes of the Center, small green apples kept falling. Above the heads of industrious haymakers, birds were busy with plans for second broods. The cycle of the year was high.*                                                                        1987

How our weather changes rapidly in Vermont; from mid-June, 1979:

*Mark Twain's words about New England weather proved true last week - "I have counted 136 different kinds of weather inside of four-and-twenty hours."*

*Tuesday was cold, windy and overcast, with a wind chill factor of only 18 degrees at one time. On Wednesday the temperature hit 34 degrees and there was scattered frost on Thursday. But the next three days made up for this cold by zooming to 90 degrees, making great haying weather.*

Some history from the mid-June 1985 column:

*Alas - the weather last week was a blot on the fair month of June - dismally cold, cloudy and showery! Such days are a rare happening for this time of year, and were the cause of much grumbling.*

*However, the memory of the June 1973 flood came to mind, when the North Randolph road was washed out and the town was designated a Federal Disaster Area. Locally a boat was sailed on the VTC campus[18] and cellars were flooded. So it could be worse now!*

*Banks of pink cinnamon roses still bloomed where they had been lovingly planted beside long-gone homes... it seemed scarcely possible that the year was at its halfway mark.*

---

[18]Vermont Technical College in Randolph Center

A description of what was blooming from 1988:

*Dainty bedstraw, a kind of wild baby's breath, bloomed across unmown fields, and the fragrance of mock orange bushes was wafted from old homesteads. Full-blown peonies and lemon lilies added their perfume to the air.*

*But black flies lurked in the shrubbery and woodchucks watched growing gardens greedily. Our Edens were fraught with perils.*

We learn about the hobblebush from 1993:

*Birds began greeting the dawn soon after 4 a.m. as the year approached its zenith. Theirs was a long day of feeding voracious offspring, with little time left for melodious arias.*

*Hobblebush flowers were striking against the low greenery of other shrubs. Their large, white clusters are sterile, serving only to attract pollinators to the insignificant fertile blooms. Since they grow horizontally near the ground, the name Witch-hobble, conjures up a trap for the unwary.*

June 24-30:

*The earth was refreshed, after three and a half inches of rain fell steadily the first of last week, ending Tuesday morning. Silken strands of spider web joined trees and bushes in Wednesday morning's heavy fog. This was the hottest day of the week, followed by two breezy, cool ones.*

*Another steady, gentle rain began falling Friday afternoon. We were fortunate to get it without accompanying winds - or even hail.*

*Daisies dotted waste spaces, interspersed with yellow and red hawkweed, (paintbrush), and patches of pink fleabone. Woodchucks made inroads on thriving gardens, tadpoles wriggled about in their watery homes and killdeer cried on high, night and day.*

*It was high summer, and hammocks made fine resting places as June took its place in history.*                                                                 1987

The same week in 1979 was down-right chilly:

*Shades of 1816, the year dubbed "eighteen hundred and froze-to-death" when frosts occurred every month of the year! There was frost in Randolph June 25, the coldest such day officially recorded in the state, with frost predicted for the following day. The weekend produced wintry weather with winds more than 20 mph adding to the chill... 1816 conditions were caused by the result of a volcanic eruption. Some scientists believe that present-day chilling had man-made causes.*

The year at its peak, from 1985:

*For a brief while, the year poised at its zenith. Bird songs were hushed as parents were occupied with their young. The shade of tall maples was refreshing, and there was joy in being at one with the season.*

Noting the changes to our landscape, from 1986:

*Ridge upon ridge of majestic blue mountains stretched forth under the bright sun early last week as summer came into its own…. The smell of freshly cut grass was becoming more familiar than that of new mown hay, as lawns multiplied and farmland diminished.*

From 1989:

*At the beginning of last week locust petals drifted down like snow from their lofty heights. It was the sweetest time of year, with the fragrance of roses, mock orange, peonies or lilies on the breeze everywhere.*

*Unmown fields were growing up to goldenrod and lacy bedstraw, while there were patches of purple vetch along the roadsides. All growth was rushing ahead pell mell, with the weeds winning every time.*

Finally, some serious flooding from 1998:

*Shades of the '27 Flood! Nearly seven inches of rain fell Thursday and Friday nights, causing flash flooding that will go down in history. The sudden devastation was incredible. Ground already saturated from last week's downpours sent tons of drenching rainfall cascading downhill in all directions. Roads, culverts, driveways and bridges were washed out in the resulting calamity.*

*It is interesting to note that the '27 Flood was caused by nine inches of rain under similar conditions. Once again, the supremacy of nature over man was incontrovertibly demonstrated…*

# July

July is the pinnacle of summer, beginning with flag waving and picnics over the Fourth, warm days filled with outdoor recreation and swimming and much outdoor work, including raspberry picking and caring for our gardens' hopefully prolific production. If we can take vacation and it is warm, we can slow time down just a bit; there is something special about swinging on a hammock, reading a novel or just taking a snooze. The following four summer weeks summarize the best of Mim's July columns; there is a brief break at the midpoint which coincides with the *Herald's* usual vacation edition.

July 1-7:

*Last week marked the beginning of real summer weather, as the prolonged spell of cold and rainy days came to an abrupt end. The full moon rising like a plump apricot was a beautiful sight on clear nights. Fireflies flitted about over dark lawns and roadsides, and nighthawks sounded.*

*Hot and humid was the order of the day, with generous amounts of rain on Wednesday and the weekend. For the fortieth year [however], the Randolph Independence Day parade was held without rain, a remarkable record. It was the first week this season that swimming places were thronged.*

*Strawberry shortcakes, band concerts and fragrant roses were among the many delights of July.*                                                                                    1985

Some weather history spanning three centuries from an early July, 1980 column:

*A look at past weather conditions shows that cold weather still prevailed in 1780, [with conditions not warming] until July 10. But in 1880 there were pleasant days for playing croquet, with just enough rain. Our own Fourth of July [1980] was blessed with cloudless skies, and the sun shone brightly on multitudes of flags and family gatherings...*

*For generations, Vermonters have felt that heaven must be an extension of the lovely, cloud-dappled Green Mountains at this time of year.*

Another heat wave began in early July, 1988 during a summer that proved to be one of the warmest on record to that time:

*Perfect summer weather graced the Fourth of July, which proved to be the beginning of another heat wave. Day after day the sun relentlessly beat down on farms and towns: not a breeze was stirring and not a drop of rain fell....*

*Humidity grew steadily worse as the East baked in the second drought of the season.[19] All creatures sought refuge from the blazing sun - birds in deep thickets, insects under stones and logs, and humans in the old swimming hole. Or, according to the legend in my childhood home, the 350-pound son of a Revolutionary soldier found relief down cellar near the cider barrel!*

---

[19]Editor's note:  Highs all week were in the 80s to the mid 90s.

Do summer days go by faster than winter ones? Early July, 1989:

*Contrary to scientific belief, summer days with 15 hours of daylight sun seem to go faster than winter ones with only ten hours of possible sunshine. There is a sense of urgency in the air, of much to be accomplished in a limited time, that is shared by every growing thing and creature.*

More on summer heat with a ditty from 1993:

*The story of last week was burned into our memories as "Hot, Hotter and Hottest." We had quite happily existed for two years without such a long stretch of hazy, hot and humid weather. In fact, we longingly remembered that blankets were required for comfortable sleeping every night last summer.*

*Homes became shuttered havens from the sun's relentless heat. Only a puny sprinkle on Thursday fell on parched lawns and gardens. Under such oppressive conditions, an old ditty came to mind:*

> *When it gets too hot for swimming,*
> *And you can't get ice cream cones,*
> *It ain't no sin to take off your skin*
> *And sit around in your bones.*

July 8 - 14:

*Cloud shadows lay like caresses on our verdant hills and valleys in last week's gorgeous summer weather. This was the high point of the year, when nights were cool enough for sleeping and days were pleasantly warm and sunny.*

*All but last Monday, when[we were] drenched in a downpour and jolted with thunder and lightning twice, killing a nearby cow. However, we had none of the hailstones which pelted other areas, fortunately.*

*Nature's roadside gardens showcased tall, rose pink fireweed and low-growing yellow bird's foot trefoil. Green regiments of corn marched over the fields, growing taller by the day. It was a time to store away not only hay and berries, but also clear golden memories to brighten the bleak days of winter which inevitably lie ahead of us all.*

1989

From the second week of July, 1979:

*For the entire past week, the weather was monotonous - hazy, hot and humid, without a break. Day after day the sun scorched its way through the skies while we earthlings utilized many ingenious ways to make life more bearable.*

A paragraph from mid July, 1980:

*As the summer reaches its height, there is a sense of satisfaction in the storing of baled hay, the neatness of well-kept lawns, [and] the fruition of carefully tended gardens. "To everything there is a season and a time for every purpose under heaven."[20]*

---

[20]Ecclesiastes 3:1.

More warm weather from 1987:

*With the exception of Tuesday, last week's weather story could be told in three sizzling letters - HOT! However, it may be mentioned that temperatures in this hilltop village never seem to be quite as high as in the valleys on these scorching days. But the general effect was wilting as the heat wave continued...*

*Roadside scenery was changing to include patches of vivid pink fireweed and blue vetch, plus stretches of lacy yellow wild parsnip. Raspberry bushes were dripping with ruby jewels, and all nature was hastening toward fruition.*

Shoeless weather described in 1994:

*This was barefoot weather, when the grass was cool beneath each toe in the morning, and sand offered inviting warmth later in the day...The sheer pleasure of stepping outdoors without having to bundle up from head to foot is a benefit of the season not to be forgotten...*

*Making a wish when you see a load of hay was an old- time custom. Now, as numerous loads of hay are passing, many of our wishes have already come true.*

July 18-24:

*Like ever-widening ripples on a pond, the days of our summer have been increasing. As the hot, sunny weather continued, night-prowling skunks riddled lawns in search of grubs.*

*After fourteen days without precipitation, a welcome rain fell last Thursday night, accompanied by strong winds and broken branches. Friday was a clear, windy day, blowing away the languor of the past.*

*Gardens which had been demanding weeding began to clamor for harvesting. And in the contentment of picking peas or berries, the sensations of summer surrounded us. There was the purring of a light plane across the sky, the buzzing of a nearby lawn mower, the fragrance of pink milkweed blossoms drifting by and the sight of exuberant children in swings.* 1983

On hailstorms past and present, from 1980:

*The damaging hailstorm [last week], which we escaped locally, did bring to light some interesting information. On June 22, 1906, hailstones fell in Chelsea over an area of one-by-ten miles "with drifts two feet deep," destroying most crops. So it could have been worse!*

From the warm summer of 1987:

*The summer of 1987 will surely go down in history as one of the hottest, and last week's weather only contributed to that distinction. Heat lightning flickered by night and humidity soared by day, with Friday claiming the dubious title of Most Uncomfortable Day...*

*Though skeletons of dead elm trees have been dominating the scene more and more, it is sad to see living specimens succumbing to the fatal disease branch by branch.*

From Mim's raspberry patch in 1990:

*Last week's weather was observed from the depth of a 50-year-old raspberry patch, which was by turns, hot and sticky, overcast and breezy, or drenched by sudden rain. From such an outpost, the querulous calling of a nuthatch could be heard as he headed down a tree trunk. In the distance young crows were trying out their adolescent voices, and overhead a kingbird's cry shrilled, as he spied the berries, no doubt.* [21]

Comparing 1999 to summers in the 1940s:

*What a summer this has been! There have been more sunny days (and more hot nights) than any other year in recent memory. Of course, the summers of '47, '48 and '49 were scorchers too, but they require a long memory.*

*The dryness continues to trouble us, as too many days go by without rain. Everything has been ahead of normal, with flowers practically racing to bloom, and then going by. The small sunflowers of black-eyed Susans and the dainty whiteness of Queen's lace decorated roadsides, while closer to home the vivid shades of phlox appeared.*

July 25-31:

*In retrospect, last week's weather seemed to be a series of showers, some light with a rainbow ending, and some torrential downpours with accompanying thunder. At first, Tuesday's precipitation was quite welcome, as lawns began a comeback from tan to green.*

*Temperatures had dropped on Monday, but Wednesday and Thursday found the hot sun beating down on berry patch and pickers. Swallows swooped low for their insect meals, and occasional breezes brought the fragrance of pink globes of milkweed flowers.*

*Many roadsides were lined with Queen Anne's lace, a dainty flower with a gory legend. The dark red center of the lacy bloom was supposed to represent a drop of blood on the ruff of beheaded Anne of Boleyn.*

*Fog surrounded us many mornings, highlighting spider webs scattered across the grass.* 1993

From the last week of July, 1980:

*But between the rains there has been a stampede of growth through the hot days. Gardens are bursting with ripening crops, and raspberry bushes tempt with ruby-laden branches. The pink glow of fireweed has replaced orange patches of day lilies along the roadsides. A veil of blue haze lies softly on the distant hills, and gentle breezes stir the leaves.*

*These are the days to dream of when winter winds howl and snow drifts deep.*

---

[21]Editor's note: I have since had the pleasure of joining Mim in her now 70 year old prolific raspberry patch which she has tended faithfully over the course of the last 5 decades. It is true that you can observe and hear much while in the process of picking berries.

Noting the near record heat from the summer of 1988:

*This summer will certainly go down in history as outstandingly hot. Hazy, hot and humid was the standard weather description, with scarcely a breeze all week. By contrast, some summers have been positively cold, notably 1956 and 1960 in recent times.*

*There were thundershowers Tuesday and Thursday, but we have had surprisingly few, considering the heat. The summer of 1953 was peppered with lightning strikes in the Center...*

Mim's philosophical viewpoint from 1986:

*As the world turns, berries ripen visibly with each day and flowers stretch upward to bloom. So the turning of the world brings maturity to us all, imperceptibly but surely.*

# August

The last full month of calendar summer in Vermont can offer a variety of temperature conditions - from a steaming heat wave to the first cool hints of early autumn. The tropical storm season edges towards this part of the world, and although Vermont is north of most of the direct impacts, its hills can land within the end point of tropical associated downpours of heavy rain. Many folks travel on vacation before the inevitable reopening of school, which over the years has moved almost imperceptibly to late August from its once traditional post-Labor Day weekend opening. Consequently, the columns from August include everything from heat and heavy rain to the first signs of the "changing of the guard"; the return of the yellow school bus, and its foretelling of the inevitable change to autumn.

August 1-7:

*After nearly three weeks of uninterrupted hot weather had practically inured us to the heat, temperatures dropped to a more bearable range. Productivity of hens and humans alike had been decreased because of the humidity and extreme warmth.*

*Cricket chirpings form an almost unnoticed background cushion these days. Queen Anne's lace decks the highways, but a portent of fall has crept into the scene as clumps of goldenrod gleam in the sun.*

*Yellow Transparent apples drop from the trees at their appointed time and thorny blackberry brambles lure the unwary. Harvesting has begun in earnest under the clear skies and gentle breezes which have replaced the haze and heat of past weeks.* 1979

From the first week of August, 1985:

*...Stately hollyhocks displayed their rosettes of red, white, pink and burgundy against domestic backgrounds, while the smell of ripening yellow Transparent apples came from nearby. We were reminded that, "While earth remains, seedtime and harvest, cold and heat, summer and winter, shall not cease.*[22]

On the hastening of the season from 1991 and 92:

*Among the bounties of the season we sometimes forget the freshness of laundry dried on the line under blue skies, or the birdsong heard through open windows... Summer has scarcely given us time to catch our breath, and already, goldenrod, a symbol of fall, is brightening the roadsides. Each remaining day is precious.*

From early August, 1994:

*...The chirping of crickets and the shrilling of cicadas replaced springtime's ardent bird songs, and sunset each evening sliced off a bit more daylight. Along roadsides were patches of hot pink fireweed, stretches of dusty pink Joe-Pye-weed, and borders of short rose beige rabbit's foot clover. Rows of once-green cornfields were tasseled out like neatly combed blond hair, when viewed from above.*

*Chilly nights were a reminder that fall was lurking in the wings.*

---

[22]Genesis 8:22

49

August 8 - 15:

*Until Friday, last week's weather was a mixture of clouds and sunshine, but then, glory be, it rained - and rained - and rained. More gentle precipitation followed on the weekend, to the great relief of us all.*

*Burdocks, thistles and beggar's lice, all villains of the plant world, were sending forth their prickly blossoms. On sunny afternoons the sound of cicadas pierced the stillness, and crickets increased their chirping as the days grew warmer. Morning after morning, the sun was retreating southward from its northernmost position in June.*

*"To everything there is a season, and a time for every purpose under heaven," and this was the time for reaping the bounty of our good earth. Fruit and flowers, grain and grasses, all have yielded their best in this season of long sunny days.*     1991

On the skies and pace of summer, 1979:

*Bright blue skies and a clear atmosphere heighten the views on every hand, from distant mountain ranges to nearby nodding sunflowers. Summer has a way of speeding on which winter never seems to do!*

From the second week of August, 1987:

*Masked bandits of the coon clan were plotting raids into cornfields in the pale moonlight. Patches of spearmint and bee balm grew high, wide and handsome, and it was time to dry their leaves for use as teas.*

From the middle of a heat wave in mid-August, 1988:[23]

*It was wall-to-wall heat again last week as the hot, humid weather continued longer than we had thought possible. Those whose memories go back 40 years will recall the roasting summer of 1949 as 1988's only rival.*

*Despite hot, dry days, blackberry patches were laden with jet-black jewels of delectable sweetness. Crickets shrilled in the background and cicadas pierced the afternoon stillness.*

*Down at the lake, [Lake Champagne] a majestic blue heron flapped solemnly over the water and barn swallows swooped in one last fly-catching fling before taking off for South America...*

Mim already noted some changes by mid-August, 1993:

*Even the birds sensed a change in the scene. Swallow families twittered on telephone wires, readying for an early migration. And where were the robins? [They were] regrouping in the woodlands.*

*Goldenrod blooming on the hillsides gave a hint of fall, and annuals were in their glory. Snapdragons, asters, calendulas and impatience made cheerful splashes of color.*

*Tranquil afternoons at the lake were numbered, and treasured accordingly. In the stillness of the night, prowling foxes barked, as the circling year rolled onward.*

---

[23]Eleven days in a row with highs in the mid to upper 80s and lows in the 60s.

August 16-23:

*Beginning with the hottest May on record, this growing season has provided more than the usual amount of Vitamin D. Glistening blackberries continued to reward the well-armored picker, as summer weather still held sway.*

*Wiry-stemmed fall dandelions cropped up on lawns, as did a variety of fly-by-night mushrooms.*

*After a delightful day, the Perseid meteors were clearly visible late Monday night. Wednesday's early red sun failed to produce the expected rain, which held off through ever-hotter days, until Sunday morning. Then the relief from humidity was slight, until a down-pour in the afternoon. When that subsided, the air was refreshingly clear and cooler.*

*Tinges of color in stressed maples here and there were an indication of things to come.* 1991

Mim tracked new pests and plants, many of which we are now (unfortunately) accustomed to; an example from 1987:

*...Sky-blue blossoms of chicory continued along roadsides elsewhere, but hadn't made it up the hill to this village. However, Japanese beetles had managed to scale the heights and riddle the community for their first devastating summer.*

*Blackberry bushes had never been more laden with luscious fruit, nor defended by fiercer thorns. Meanwhile, wild cucumbers with frothy white flowers vaulted stone walls and scrambled over bushes.*

*Hot, humid days, of which we've had more than usual this summer, ended the week on a high note...*

From the warm summer of 1995:

*It seemed inconceivable that we could be suffering three months of such heat and humidity, but such has been the case. This summer, which will go down in history as the hottest summer in memory, reached its pinnacle Thursday when the heat index was 105 degrees! (Remember, this figure is determined by humidity and air temperature.)*

*Fortunately, humidity decreased as the week wore on, though there was not a drop of rain, and hardly a breeze. Clouds dappled the hillsides and green regiments of corn grew ever taller.*

*Birds of a feather were flocking together, wheeling and swooping over fields. The feathers were black, belonging to starlings, redwings, grackles and cowbirds holding family reunions before their time of migration.*

One more paragraph on blackberries from mid-August, 1995:

*It was the time of juicy blackberries, the fruit of remembrance. For some, they represent thorny berry-picking excursions in childhood, and for others, perhaps an encounter with a bear in the patch. So nature, weather and memory sometimes blend in an enduring scene.*

August 24-31:

*Veils of blue haze almost obscured the distant mountains, as hot and humid days held sway last week. Our belated summer weather had arrived just as school was beginning, and swimming was most tempting.*

*Cornfields rustled in the gentle breeze and tam-o'-shanter acorns were dropping on the path to school. It was going to be a good year for butternuts, whose sticky green husks were used for a khaki dye in the old days.*

*Saturday brought an abrupt change in the weather, with sunshine and shadow alternating and cool breezes blowing. Sunflowers nodded on their tall stalks, as six hawks soared together high in the sky, like a constellation.*

*Days were as short as they had been in April, and summer memories had all been harvested.*
1992

From 1986:

*"To everything there is a season, and a time for every purpose under heaven... a time to plant, a time to reap,"[24] and we have been reaping - fruits and grains and sun-lit memories to brighten the long winter ahead.*

The tropical storm season was underway, but at the same time the first hints of fall were as well, from 1991:

*Like many of the dreaded disasters of life, the fury of Hurricane Bob passed us by Monday, leaving only much needed rainfall. [However], it wasn't until Thursday that the sun deigned to shine on us again. In fact, the warmth of the kitchen stove had felt downright good...*

*Clusters of pinkish seeds hung from boxelders like blossoms, tam-o'-shanter acorns were littering the ground and glossy buckeyes split their massive overcoats to intrigue passing youngsters. There was an almost fall-feeling in the air.*

From 1996:

*Conditions were perfect for picking this season's abundant crop of glistening blackberries to a cricket chorus. Each golden day was savored like a juicy peach. Yet, waiting in the wings were droves of yellow school buses, heralding the coming of fall to these hills and valleys.*

School had just begun in the last week of August, 1997:

*Never mind what the calendar says! When yellow school buses start driving down our country roads, fall begins in Vermont. It represents a changing of the guard, so to speak. Foggy mornings were the distinguishing characteristic of back-to-school days with a mixture of sun and clouds later....*

*Days were getting dark sooner than we'd like, yet the equinox was still ahead of us. Nature was giving us time for harvesting both the yields of our gardens and warm memories against the coming winter.[25]*

---

[24]Ecclesiastes 3:1-2

[25]Editor's note: before moving from August to September I must also applaud Mim's high degree of interest in our environment. In her August 29, 1985 column she announced that she would begin giving pH readings for rainfall and she gave a summary of the pollutants causing the problem. She concluded with:

"In the Adirondacks 264 lakes are now devoid of fish life because of acid rain, while six in Vermont are endangered and 20 more are critical."

# September

SEPTEMBER IS THE TRANSITION TIME TO AUTUMN. GARDENERS ARE WATCHING CAREFULLY FOR THE FIRST FROST AND BIRDERS ARE WATCHING HAWKS SOARING AS MANY OF OUR SUMMER BIRD FRIENDS ARE DEPARTING. FOG IS THE DOMINANT MORNING THEME. THE BIGGEST LANDSCAPE CHANGE, OF COURSE, IS THE COLOR, WHICH MIM DESCRIBES BEAUTIFULLY EACH YEAR. TO OPEN SEPTEMBER, 1995 MIM QUOTED FROM HELEN HUNT JACKSON:

"THE GOLDENROD IS YELLOW,
THE CORN IS TURNING BROWN,
THE TREES IN APPLE ORCHARDS
WITH FRUIT ARE BENDING DOWN...

BY ALL THESE LOVELY TOKENS
SEPTEMBER DAYS ARE HERE,
WITH SUMMER'S BEST OF WEATHER
AND AUTUMN'S BEST OF CHEER."

September 1-7:

"How swift the summer goes,
Forget-me-not, pink, rose,
The young grass when I started
And now the hay is carted."

With Masefield we can echo the poignancy of summer's passing. Days have continued cool and crisp.

When was the last chimney swift, so prominent in summer skies, seen? Without fanfare, our feathered summer residents slip away as it grows colder.

Summertime's green hillsides had a yellowish cast last week, with here and there reddish spots, as leaves began their transformation to a tapestry of vivid hues.

It is a late season indeed when a dishful of raspberries can be picked in September. In 1988 the last picking here was on August 5. Perhaps this augurs for a long-lasting fall like 1970 when there was no frost until November.                    1989

Some notes on the changing scene from 1982 and 1998:

The appearance of school busses on country roads signals the beginning of fall to Vermonters, who might as well devise a calendar of their own. Fall dandelions dot green lawns, and late arrivals like swallows and hummingbirds depart unnoticed. Asters appear like lavender smoke on the roadsides...

Birds of a feather were flocking together - the feathers were black and the birds were grackles and starlings, red-wings and cowbirds, swooping over cornfields in rehearsals for their flight south.

On the Jerusalem artichoke, 1986:

*Along old roadsides are the small sunflower blossoms of Jerusalem artichoke, whose tubers Champlain took back to Europe as a delicacy in the 1600's. Indians and early settlers enjoyed them, and present day cooks are beginning to appreciate their flavor, too.*

And it can still be plenty warm in early September, 2001:

*Slowly but surely, the sun was creeping southward, leaving us with fewer minutes of daylight and also cooler temperatures... (But) by Friday it was summer all over again. Saturday the temperature hit 90 degrees, reminiscent of 1960, when September 9 was the hottest day of the year.*

September 8-15:

*Flashes of sunshine were the best we could hope for last week, as clouds darkened most days, and showers fell sporadically. It was windy enough to break off a few branches, and chilly, too, hinting strongly of things to come.*

*Diminutive hummingbirds still frequented their favorite flowers, but many varieties of birds had left an emptiness in bushes and trees as they silently departed. Chipmunks peered warily from stonewalls where their winter stores were accumulating.*

*Rose-hued buckeye burrs were shaken from their trees, revealing the glossy brown treasures school children have collected for countless years.*

*Here and there a fiery red maple tree stood out like a soloist before the approaching crescendo of fall's symphony of color. It was a time of high anticipating.*     1994

We were into the season when tropical storm remnants could occasionally cause havoc, this far north and inland, from 1979:

*Tropical storm David left a wake of broken limbs, branches and leaves strewn over lawns and roads on Thursday.*

*"When the wind is from the East.*
*It's neither good for man nor beast."*

*Thursday began with winds up to 40 m.p.h. from the east and torrential rain, but ended with the usual westerly wind and clearing skies. The lunar eclipse, which occurred in the early morning hours, was hidden from view by fog, though the evening before the moon rose in the sky like a misty apricot.*

From 1980:

*Tomatoes gleam like jewels on the bony fingers of their vines, and fragrant apples weigh down the orchard branches. Animals and humans alike are diligently harvesting all that can be found, in preparation for the long winter ahead.*

*A prowling fox barks hoarsely in the moonless night, and crickets chirp, as one more circling year draws nearer to its close.*

On the first frost dates, 1982, 1996:

*We were equally fortunate not to have been touched by frost; though the average date of first frost hereabouts comes around the autumnal equinox. There have been times when tender growing things were nipped the first week of September, and then there was one memorable year when no frost touched our fair land until November first! (1970).*

*After days when scattered frosts were warned and a fire in the kitchen stove felt good, we were suddenly back in the warm lap of summer Friday. Temperatures rose into the eighties...*

Mim was less than thrilled when snow came early in 1986:

*The weather provided a better than usual topic of conversation last week. It was sunny but breezy Monday, followed by rain after dark and - horrors - snow in upper elevations! This on September 16. Wind chill Tuesday was around 20 degrees at times, and out came the woolies before summer had even officially ended. Although frost threatened Wednesday morning, wind and clouds combined to avert this calamity...*[26]

On the frequent September morning fog, from 2000:

*Long after our morning fog had disappeared and the sun was shining brightly, we could look down toward the valleys to the east and to the west, and see fog boiling up like witches' cauldrons. Ah, the advantages of living on a mountaintop, where the wind blows strongest and the sun lasts longest!*

News overshadowed the weather in September 2001:

*On Tuesday (9/11) we were hardly aware of the weather, so stunned and devastated were we over the horrific tragedies in New York and Washington. It was reported to be sunny and pleasant.*

*Skies were cloudless and peaceful Wednesday morning, and our thoughts were with the equally innocent and unsuspecting thousands whose morning had begun in a similar manner the day before. Our world had been changed forever in a matter of minutes.*

September 16-23:

*Hot, hazy and humid weather, which had eluded us all during the summer, was here for three balmy days last week. Gardens burst forth with ripening vegetables and gloriously vivid flowers. Rain fell only at night.*

*The weekend brought an abrupt change to clear, crisp days, so perfect for fair- going. Color-touched hillsides extended into vistas of ridge upon ridge of blue mountains.*

*Squirrels frisked about in their search for winter provisions, and even black bears were seen, fattening up against the cold months ahead. In the meanwhile, we humans were storing up memories of golden days, as we added to the woodpile and cooked up another batch of spicy pickles.* 1992

---

[26]Editor's note: Mim also noted that worse things could happen, citing David Ludlum's book on Vermont weather; [*The Vermont Weather Book*, 1985] which noted an 8-10 inch snowfall in Randolph on the 23rd of September, 1885.

On the early start to the foliage season in 1981:

*Color is licking at the hills like a grassfire spreading over the countryside. Where last year the foliage was late in coloring up, it seems to be earlier than usual this year. All growing things are being caught up in the vivid pageant of autumn.*

On the 50th anniversary of a hurricane, 1988:

*There were those whose memories went back 50 years to the unexpected hurricane of Sept. 21, 1938, which wreaked havoc this far inland, uprooting mighty trees at the Center and bringing all activities to a standstill. The possibility of another such disaster always exists.*

On the first frost, from 1993:

*The first killing frost is often regarded with the same stoicism that greets the appearance of the first gray hair; it was inevitable, but the later, the better. And so it was Monday morning, as we ruefully surveyed white lawns, blackened squash vines and a multitude of tender flowers in ruin. Although summer did not officially end until Wednesday, it was long gone as far as we were concerned.*

From 1994:

*Hillsides were showing a hundred shades of yellow and orange, brown and scarlet, warming up for the grand explosion of color which brings the growing season to a triumphal conclusion.*

*Conditions have been just right for a bumper nut crop this year. Beechnuts, hazelnuts, hickory nuts and butternuts, all are bearing abundantly. Farm wives used butternut husks for a brown dye even within memory.*

On fog and advancing frost from 1995:

*Fog, the trademark of fall, came boiling up from the valleys like witches' brew, last week. On Tuesday frost whitened the fields, creeping closer to our dwellings like a predator stalking its prey....*

*The earthy fragrance of ripening apples was as beguiling to us as it must have been to our earliest ancestors. And so we faced harsher times, well supplied with pies and sauce and memories.*

Reviewing Hurricane Floyd from 1999:

*... such idyllic weather came crashing to an end with Hurricane Floyd's remnants on Thursday. Heavy rains, which we had been denied for at least four months, drenched us thoroughly. Rivers low enough to walk across the day before became raging torrents, prompting flood warnings.*

*High winds [up to 51 mph] tore across hills and valleys, toppling trees and knocking out power to hundreds. Schools to the north and south, east and west, were closed on Friday, all except Randolph, it seemed.*

*Chainsaws were buzzing, sawing up a winter's supply of fallen wood, in some cases. But parched and panting Mother Earth was abundantly refreshed, and the sun shone brightly on Saturday and Sunday to dry out the soggy ground and cheer the crews who were picking up the pieces left by Hurricane Floyd.*

September 24-30:

*Like frosting on the cake of the year came the overwhelmingly beautiful display covering hills and valleys. Fall foliage peaked fully a week early this season, and in Wednesday's welcome sunshine, the reds were especially glorious to behold.*

*With Edna St. Millay, we could exclaim, "O World, I cannot hold thee close enough!"*

*Bluebirds warbled through the fog last Monday morning, and later the sun glistened on long strands of spider webs. By night it was raining, and Tuesday was a wet day. But blue and gold weather followed.*

*A peach-tinted sunrise Sunday morning highlighted the golden leaves, which were starting to fall. Silhouettes of butternut trees were bereft of foliage, while locusts were still verdant, yet each was proceeding down its own path toward winter.*        1986

From late September, 1979:

*Here and there a maple tree-crimson or fiery orange-stands out like a soloist before the approaching crescendo of fall's symphony of color. Once more the hills are tuning up for this most spectacular season of the year...*

The change of colors arrived at different times over the years; from late September, 1980:

*Flocks of wild geese honked their way across cold, clear skies Saturday as chilling winds blew steadily... Foliage is much later in turning than last year. Still green trees appear to be waiting for some invisible signal before rolling out the red carpet for autumn's triumphant entry.*

On apples from late September, 1982:

*Now the gnarled trees in abandoned orchards bravely bring forth their fruit for deer or cattle only. Their names are evocative of the past, when each had a virtue of its own - Pewaukee, Pippin, Tolman Sweet, Tetoski, Wolf River, and Bethel.*

Two astronomical highlights noted from 1996:

*The highlight of last week was definitely Thursday, beginning with a colorful flash of light and explosive sound early in the morning. A meteor is the accepted explanation of this phenomenon. Then that evening provided perfect viewing conditions for the last total lunar eclipse of the century. Jonathan Carpenter made the first recorded observation of such an event here on November 11, 1780.*

Birding in late September, 1999:

*Friday was the ideal time for a picnic on a high hill, watching hawks soar effortlessly on the thermals. Snow geese honked their way across the sky, while Canada geese landed in fields.*

# October

This is the month of autumn, a beautiful season as well as a major transition month, when cold air begins its assault once again on the Vermont landscape. The first of the white stuff usually falls in these hills in the latter portion of the month. Of course, the peaking of the fall foliage season is arguably Vermont's natural highlight of the year, drawing hundreds of thousands of tourists annually. The timing for the peak is impacted by temperature and soil moisture levels, but it usually arrives within the first two weeks of the month. Predicting its duration and intensity remains one of Vermont's mysteries, on a par with the sugaring season in late winter and early spring. October also features the final autumnal harvest, and folks are completing outdoor chores and stacking wood if not done already in preparation for the long winter ahead. The month ends with the annual celebration of Halloween, when our children go out here in the Center visiting neighbors while receiving goodies, and often learning more about the local history of this unique place.

*October 1-7:*

*Wave after wave of brilliance swept down across the countryside, covering our beloved hills with the beauty of a medieval tapestry. Wherever we look, each bush and fern and tree is adding its bit to the splendor of the scene.*

*Crimson maples, golden birches and russet ash contrast vividly with the evergreens. Advancing in the face of snow and cold, autumn is flaunting its colors in a final triumphant show, before surrendering to the bleakness of winter.*

*A killing white frost clamped its jaws on tender growing things last Monday. Nights are longer and birds are flocking, reminding us that every sunny fall day is a dividend.* 1980

From the history archives on early snow; 1981:

*Though snow is visible on distant ski slopes, old-time Center residents can remember that, on Sept. 25, 1950, the ground was white with snow. Yet within a week, the hottest day on record occurred! So the chance of lovely October days is still very possible.*

On the beautiful color from 1982:

*Whole hillsides flamed with the breath-taking beauty of gold, orange and red leaves. Yet the splendor of a single sun-sparkled poplar could thrill the senses equally. Appearing as faithfully as the promised rainbow, this matchless display of nature comes as a benediction to the year.*

On an early snow from the first week of October, 1987:

*The bad news came Sunday, which began with driven rain, later turning to bouncing hail and then settling down to a heavy, windblown snow. Saturday's rain had deposited many leaves on the ground, but the next day snow-laden branches tumbled down as well. Seven or eight inches of snow caused widespread damage.*

*Such abominable weather is, unfortunately, not without precedent. The day after the famous Royalton Raid on Oct. 16, 1780 eight inches of snow fell as captives were marched off to Canada. On Oct. 10, 1925 a howling blizzard brought over a foot of drifting snow before farmers had finished harvesting corn and potatoes. Only eight years ago two or three inches of snow whitened the ground and draped still-bright leaves.*

Some poetry from 1991:
*Saturday's pouring rain brought down the curtain, cold and gray, on foliage viewing. Nature was narrowing our personal world to four walls of security against harsher elements.*

> *Wild geese wing through the cold night skies*
> *Uttering their plaintive, haunting cries*
> *Till even my earthbound soul replies*
> *To their cadence of freedom that swells and dies*[27]

On the circle of time from 1996:
*The importance of home and hearth loomed large in our lives, as the weather drove us indoors, and nights grew longer. The circling year had arrived at a time of counting our blessings, not only for warmth and nourishment and shelter, but for the rich harvest of friendships and enriching experiences.*

October 8-15:
*Last Monday was blustery, with a few snowflakes in the air, but to the north some folks found as much as 11 inches of snow on the ground! It was the end of all tender growing things Tuesday morning, when a killing frost whitened the grass. Loosened by the cold, leaves came sifting down, making an ankle-deep carpet that rustled underfoot and smelled of fall.*

*All was not lost, for we were treated next to a spell of Indian summer. Delightfully warm days followed, just right for one more picnic, with the distant hills a lovely blue. The blazing colors, so intense we could not bear to view them indefinitely, had softened appreciably, like a fire settling down to a warm glow.*

*"Weatherwise" has just passed its 23rd birthday of celebrating the weather. Here is a quote from one of the earlier columns:*

*"A prowling fox barks hoarsely in the moonless night, and crickets chirp, as one more circling year draws nearer to its close."*                    2001

From 1979:
*Wild geese flying across a harvest moon honk their plaintive farewells, stirring our hearts with the poignancy of the passing year.*

---

[27]Miriam Herwig, 1991

Another natural phenomenon from October, 1983:

*It started with a mighty rumbling early Friday morning and soon developed into a full-fledged earthquake, shaking walls and rattling dishes. Centered in the Adirondacks, its magnitude was 5.2, greater than last year's Jan. 18 quake, which measured 4.8 on the Richter scale but was centered in Franklin, N.H.*

*Although many citizens were jolted awake by the tremor, there was tangible evidence down on Route 14, where a tree toppled onto an electric line, causing a power loss northward.*[28]

Winter tried to come in early in the second week of October, 1986:

*Last Monday was a shocker! Trees writhed and parted with branches in the raging winds which never let up all day. There was snow in the air and the chill factor was down to 10 degrees. Between the night's rain and the constant gusts, no semblance of beautiful colors was left on the trees...*

*The glittering white of frost on every side greeted our eyes Saturday morning and again on Sunday. The green world was coming to an end. Color was drained from the trees, returning to the earth from whence it came.*

More from the second week of October, 1992:

*Last week the Center maples burst into orange torches, brightening our days. Lesser foliage, in shades from russet to saffron, crowded fall's magnificent canvas. But by week's end a carpet of gold lay on the ground. Rain had begun dislodging this fleeting display of grandeur...*

*The full moon shone down on a rich scene - corn fields being harvested, heaps of fat pumpkins and homes being battened against the coming winter. Life was good in the hills of Vermont.*

Not every autumn was quite as colorful as the norm, as seen in 1996:

*This has been a topsy turvy fall, with disappointingly drab foliage except in a few favored spots. Comments like, "I've never seen such a dull autumn before" were common, and were true in many instances.*

*However, diary research reveals that an identical situation occurred in 1961, when a hard freeze before the leaves turned color made them brown and shriveled, instead. Fortunately, that was 35 years ago, and everyone fervently hopes it will be 35 more years before it happens again.*[29]

---

[28]Editor's note: Fortunately we have not experienced serious earthquakes, but there is occasional geological movement as evidenced in 1982, 1983 and 1988.

[29]Editor's note: 2005 did not provide a very colorful season either; soil moisture levels and the lack of any significant chilly weather may have contributed. In Vermont it will always prove difficult to accurately predict the full nature or outcome of our famous foliage and sugaring seasons. Perhaps that unpredictability is something else that fortifies Vermont's people and underscores their adaptability to this special environment.

October 16-23:
*The remnants of fall foliage lie like a faded paisley shawl draped over the shoulders of the hills. Lawns are covered with a textured gold carpet of leaves, and the trees stand about in various stages of undress.*

*Snow flurries and cold winds ushered in last week and our third hard frost struck Wednesday. By Friday, the weather warmed up so nicely that outdoor chores were a real pleasure.*

*As the days grow colder, plumes of wood smoke rise from more and more chimneys, and the air is fragrant with this primitive smell of home and hearth. The Hunter's Moon rides across chilly night skies, signaling the stealthy approach of winter.* 1980

1992:
*The first snow is often greeted by the same stoicism as the appearance of the first gray hair - with the knowledge that more will follow. And last Monday we had such a covering...*

*Poplars made splashes of yellow against the rich browns of beech and oak on our hillsides. Small maples retained some of their peach-colored foliage, but daily the scene became more drab.*

Quoting Henry David Thoreau from 1994:
*Nature was embarking on her wonderfully efficient recycling, as fallen leaves blended into a collie-colored carpet. Even oak trees were letting go of their leathery brown foliage, but young maples, late to catch the fever which swept their elders a month ago, were decked out in yellow and orange.*

*Thoreau wrote of fallen leaves, "How beautifully they die, making cheerfully their annual contribution to the soil. They fall to rise again." And so we bow to winter's inevitability, knowing that spring will surely be our reward for compliance.*

On the landscape from 1995:
*Summertime secrets were revealed in the leafless branches of tall trees - gray paper bees' nests, straggly squirrels' nests and a great diversity of birds' nests... The sodden landscape showed only subdued spice colors - cinnamon frosted ferns, ginger-hued poplars and nutmeg shades of fallen leaves. Earth was being readied for its long winter nap.*

From mid-October, 1999, on global warming, after three days of Indian summer:
*It is interesting to note that last year was the hottest on record worldwide, and the four hottest years since 1860 occurred in the 1990's. When this year's stats are in, they may top all others, giving incontrovertible evidence of global warming. Its causes and results must be given high priorities on this planet we share with six billion others.*

A later foliage season; from the third week of October, 2001:
*Orange was the color of the day, as last week began. Sunlight shining through apricot-colored maples lit them up like flames in early morning, and fat pumpkins added to the scene. Even butterflies were orange, in the case of Monarchs. Hillsides*

*remained a tapestry of loveliness, even in partial undress. "Beauty is its own excuse for being" said Ralph Waldo Emerson, but we were certainly its beneficiaries.*

*By mid-week, late-bloomers of the forest were coming into their own-butter yellow for poplars and leathery brown for oak. Winds made us shiver outdoors, and stripped trees of their leaves in the reverse order that they appeared in spring.*

October 24-31:

*October's run of dry, warmer-than-average weather continued all last week, making the whole month a pleasant one to remember, as gray, rainy November days loomed ahead.*

*Saturday's rosy sunrise silhouetted leafless trees and steeples alike in fleeting beauty. Sunset that night was equally glorious, overspreading the sky with majestic, copper-hued clouds.*

*Tiny locust leaves came drifting down like green snow, and puffs of yellow poplar leaves fluttered in the breeze.*

*Disappointed blue jays found the bird bath frozen over Wednesday morning, and again on Thursday. Robins still lingered in some locales, but winter visitors like chickadees, nuthatches and woodpeckers were beginning to show up on a regular basis.*

*Along with the waning moon, the winter constellation of Orion, the hunter, could be seen in early morning skies. With the onset of standard time Sunday, and longer, darker evenings, hearth and home assumed ever greater importance.*          1994

From 1979:

*October weather demonstrated its versatility last week by ranging from record breaking heat on Monday and Tuesday to snow-covered ground and fog on Sunday...*

*Scenes of austerity on every hand remind us that winter is getting nearer. Yet here and there a determined dandelion blooms, or a hardy Johnny-jump-up shows a brave blossom in defiance of the cold.*

Describing an autumnal gale in 1980:

*Cloudiness changed to rain driven by gale force winds that blew down branches and denuded trees. Relentlessly, the wind fingered dwellings for some crevice to enter, as velocities at the Center ranged from 40 to 60 m.p.h. [yet,] enlivening the bleak landscape are patches of frosted ferns, looking like tousled, rust-colored fur.*

Quoting Robert Frost from 1981:

*This is a time for scuffing through the leaves, for turning up your collar against the chill in the wind, and for spotting flocks of south-bound geese honking through the skies...*

*Now we can echo with Robert Frost:*

> *"Ah when to the heart of man*
> *Was it ever less than a treason?*
> *To... bow and accept the end*
> *Of a love or a season?"*[30]

---

[30]*The Poetry of Robert Frost*, Edward Lathem, Editor, 1979

Speaking of a white Halloween, 1993:

*The last thing we were dreaming of was a white Halloween, but that was just what nature handed us last weekend. More than two inches of snow plastered the ground and outlined bare branches Sunday morning. Not in the memory of the oldest trick-or-treater had there been such discouraging weather.*

Late October 2000:

*After Monday's freeze had whitened the land, tiny locust leaves came sifting down through the sunlight. It was our good luck to have another spell of Indian summer, which continued right through Friday. Some years there is no such respite.*

*This was bonus time for the fabled grasshoppers among us to catch up on postponed chores, to breathe in the pungent smell of fall and scuff through the rustling leaves. The weather was great for raking those leaves into huge piles for small fry to jump in...*

# November

*The cloudiest, darkest month has its meteorological highlights. Although we are (for all practical purposes) beginning the long haul of winter, and it is likely we will experience the first substantial snow, we can still experience Indian summer. And you will see that Mim could find against the often bleak, grey background, color or some bright spot to highlight, particularly early in the month. If fortunate, we may get some mid-month clearing to view the annual Leonid meteor showers before we prepare for the holiday season, which begins with America's traditional celebration of the annual harvest at Thanksgiving.*

November 1-7:
*Thoreau wrote of fallen leaves, "How beautifully they die, making cheerfully their annual contribution to the soil. They fall to rise again."*

*Trees stripped bare of their leaves by wind and rain last week revealed summer's secrets - the nests of birds and squirrels and hornets. The scene was a somber one, as earth settled down for its long rest. Hillsides were frequently darkened by clouds, for November is the month with the least sunshine.*

*Here and there a hardy, short-stemmed dandelion bloomed in some sheltered spot, and Johnny jump-ups still showed cheerful little faces. At this time bright red high-bush cranberries make splashes of color in moist lands. It is surprising to learn that these are cousins of the snowball bush, which is showy but sterile, so bears no fruit.*
                                                                                    1991

On some unexpected warmth from early November, 1978:
*The blessing of Indian summer has lain upon the land for nine days like a warm blanket of peacefulness. Except for the danger of low water supplies for some, this is regarded as an unexpected gift, to be stored up in memory against the bitter winter days coming.*

*Ten years ago eight inches of snow fell on Nov. 7 and 8, signaling the beginning of winter, and five years ago there was snow on the ground.*

From early November, 1987:
*Occasional patches of tamaracks gleamed like orange candles against the somber hillsides. Evening grosbeaks, our star winter boarders, were back early from the north. Last year it was mid-November when they came.*

1988:
*Still showing color on otherwise subdued hillsides were the feathery gold of tamaracks and the warm brown of oaks last week...*

*Mention should be made that, for the first and only time, a hurricane was named Miriam when "she" crossed from the Atlantic, where "she" had been known as Joan, to the Pacific last Monday.*

November 8-15:

*The pace of nature was slowing down last week. No more bursts of growth or color, no sudden bird melodies filling the air. Somber grey days set the mood for quiet contemplation and indoor occupations. Sunlight was scarce, but rain drizzled down on several days and nights. Friday morning revealed a dusting of snow and fringe of tiny icicles on the bird feeder.*

*And so we progressed to the start of another hunting season. Twenty years ago it began with Indian summer and no need for longjohns. Last year was a different story, when eight inches of snow provided ideal tracking conditions. This year the momentous Saturday had run-of-the-mill weather, neither balmy nor snowy.*

*Sunday's gusty winds were certainly challenging to anyone outdoors. They were part of nature's hardening process, readying us for winter.*                    1998

Winter was coming on in mid-November 1980:

*It looked like winter, it felt like winter, [and] it sounded like winter, as the wind howled and the ground was covered with snow the first three days of last week. Wind chill factors were 20 degrees below zero at times…*

*Overhead, the Beaver Moon shines down on a stark landscape, dotted with the lights of snug homes ready for the onslaught of winter.*

More on November snow from 1986:

*Thursday was our time of baptism by snow. We awoke to the scraping of snowplows and the soft thudding of falling snow. Eight inches of white blanketing greeted our eyes… November snows of the past come to mind. On November 7, 1968 a foot of snow fell, and stayed…But the granddaddy of November snows occurred on Thanksgiving eve and day 1971 when a foot and a half of snow came down!*

Finding color through the sunrise and sunsets, 1995:

*As earth's hues grew more somber, we were rewarded by flaming sunsets and sunrises of lambent rose early in the week. "I'll tell you how the sun rose a ribbon at a time," wrote Emily Dickinson, but I'll tell you that stormy weather usually follows such times of colorful beauty. And sure enough, it was raining by Tuesday afternoon and snowing alternately.*

From 1996:

*No one can deny that Vermont has a plentiful variety of weather, with enough to go around and some to spare. Indeed, it is our standard topic of conversation, and Vermonters undoubtedly would be at a loss for words in Singapore, where the temperature varies only about four degrees.*

*Last week there was plenty to talk about weather-wise. After several cold, cloudy days, with occasional glimpses of sunshine, the temperature zoomed up on Friday to set new records for warmth, and to offer one more opportunity to do outdoor chores.*

November 16-23:

*Over the river and through the wood to Grandmother's house they came, thankful that they didn't have to travel by sleigh on the coldest day of the season so far. [On the other hand] Thanksgiving 1931 was quite the opposite of this year's chilly holiday. Extreme warmth prompted this incipient weather observer to scratch down the unusual fact on a large stone that day.*

*Sounds traveled further now that tree leaves no longer muffled them. Among the sounds to be heard were the raucous cries of blue jays and the scolding of gray squirrels.*

*As if in atonement for the depressingly cloudy weather earlier this month, the sun brightened our lives every day last week until Sunday. Then weather forecasters uttered the two words that strike fear into the hearts of pedestrians and drivers alike - "freezing rain." True to their predictions, tiny frozen pellets began bouncing off the ground like tapioca, and collecting in white areas Sunday morning. Fortunately, plain, cold rain soon took over, lessening the danger.* 2000

From 1981:

*Gray is the color of November - slate gray, lowering clouds, dove-gray distant hills and pearly gray skies. Somberness is the mood of these sunless days.*

From 1997, after 5.5" of snow fell on the weekend, Mim wrote:

*Matters could have been worse. In 1798, according to weather historian David Ludlum, three feet of snow fell in New England on Nov. 21-2-3!*

*At a time when we retreat to our shelters, it is amazing how numerous small creatures and at least a dozen and a half species of birds flourish in spite of the cold outdoors.*

On the annual Leonid meteor shower from 1998:

*Although snow deprived us of the opportunity to see the Leonid meteor shower, its most outstanding display in 1833 was viewed in Randolph Center by William Nutting. This early meteorologist lived across the street from this weather observer, who has a copy of his records. He described the wonderful sight as follows:*

*"Meteors falling in all directions and of all sizes; at any moment from 5:30 a.m. to daylight several might be seen at the same time - as daylight advanced, the atmosphere became so cloudy that they could not be seen, though, till the clouds obstructed the sight, they appeared to be moving with unabated rapidity."*

November 24-30:

*It was a wintry Thanksgiving this year, with ice encrusting ponds and slower streams. A morning reading of 2 degrees failed to warm up much, despite the sun's best efforts.*

*But 50 years ago Thanksgiving followed "the biggest November snowfall in man's memory, 2 to 3 feet, with deer hunters lost, wires down, lights off, places isolated," according to this observer's 1943 diary. It was war time, and my soldier brother had come home in a sleigh for his only leave.*

In more recent times, 1971's Thanksgiving stands out as the year a foot of snow fell, stalling traffic everywhere.

*Steadily, the march of days has been leading toward winter solstice, shortening daylight hours, to the despair of sun worshippers. Still, on some mornings, the drabness of gray-brown hillsides was relieved by vivid coral, peach and gold sunrise colors.*

*Sunday provided a change of pace, a soggy one, to be sure, as the mercury climbed, rain fell, and winds blew. Mother nature was giving the earth a good washing before putting it to sleep.*                    1993

On prior Thanksgivings from 1982:

*But oh, Thanksgivings past! In 1934 it was so warm that only sweaters were needed outdoors, while in 1939 ponds were frozen hard enough for skating. And in 1971 a foot and a half of snow fell the night before the holiday.*

From late November, 1987:

*At this time of year the eye rejoices in small bounties, like burnished sunrise clouds or the dipping flight of a chickadee, which might go only half-observed in the splendors of summer.*

*More than a dozen varieties of winter birds flock around wherever there is food and are joined by gray squirrels.*

*Like a new swimmer, cautiously testing the water, we ventured into winter weather step by step last week.*

From the end of November 1988:

*Some Center residents were shaken, while others claim to have remained untouched by last Friday evening's earthquake, which measured 6.0 on the Richter scale and was centered north of Quebec City. It was the strongest tremor in the region since 1926 - which few of us remember.*

*Previous recent tremors which were felt locally were in January 1982, measuring 4.8 and centered in Franklin, N.H., and in October 1983, measuring 5.2 and centered in the Adirondacks. When it is considered that, on the Richter scale, each step is approximately 10 times greater than the preceding step; the enormity of difference is more easily realized.*[31]

---

[31]*Editor's note: The Richter scale is logarithmic; hence each step is ten times the amplitude of the prior step - however the energy released is approximately 32 times greater for each step up on the scale.*

# December

THE WINTER SOLSTICE AND THE HOLIDAY SEASON HELP FOLKS THROUGH THE SHORTEST DAYS OF THE YEAR AND THE ACCOMPANYING COLDER WEATHER. YOU WILL NOTICE MIM'S INCREASING RELIANCE ON THE HEARTH AND HOME AND HOW THE HOLIDAY LIGHTING AND CHEER ADD TO THE WARMTH OF THE SEASON. SNOWFALL PICKS UP THIS MONTH AND WINTER TAKES CONTROL OF THE LANDSCAPE. HIGH WIND SPEEDS FROM POWERFUL STORMS ARE ALSO POSSIBLE THIS MONTH.

December 1-7:

*Goldfinches in winter garb came flitting down to feed with purple finches and tree sparrows in Tuesday's chill air. Two inches of snow fell after dark, but changed to freezing rain and then foggy rain next morning. On Thursday high winds buffeted houses all day and night - a fine time to be indoors.*

*Our eyes became more accustomed to white surroundings as the week progressed, with dustings of snow now and then. Like the mythological Proserpina, we are now in the six-month period of desolation and bleakness on earth.*

*Cheerful Christmas lights appeared to brighten the darkness and intricate frost designs graced window panes. As John Ruskin wrote, "Nature is painting for us, day after day, pictures of infinite beauty if only we have the eyes to see them."*     1986

Summarizing a severe early winter storm from December 1981:

*After a dismal fall that might better be forgotten, winter bids fair to be a season that will long be remembered for the worst December storm in 50 years. All Saturday night howling winds tore over the hills like a freight train, and blizzard conditions, with temperatures in the teens and driven snow drifting, continued all Sunday.*

*The Herwig anemometer, installed five years ago, registered higher wind velocity than ever before - 60 mph, and the blowing went on constantly.*

From 1985:

*The nearly full moon last Monday night shone down on a bitter cold scene. Constant winds had lowered the chill factor below zero. But it had been a sunny day, the only one of the week...*

*Gradually the year was winding down for its period of rest. Darkness occupied larger parts of each day and activities centered around the warmth and shelter of homes.*

On a rare winter rainbow and another Herwig anemometer wind velocity record, 1989:

*Last Tuesday was remarkable for a beautiful complete rainbow in the northeast, a rare location, because conditions conducive to its formation seldom exist when the sun is so far south in the winter.*

*That day also broke wind records for the past 14 years of anemometer observations when 72 mph was recorded. Within 24 hours there had been sleet, freezing rain, rain, sunshine and then powerful gales.*

December 8-14:

*Last week began with a burst of weather activity - fog, hail, snow, and the second highest winds of the year blowing fiercely at 58 mph. Winter had us firmly in its grip.*

*Tuesday was sunny and cold, with winds continuing up to 53 mph, producing an unmentionable chill factor.*

*Daylight hours numbered fewer than nine, which had the advantage of making sunrises, like Wednesday's peach and gold one, available to most of us.*

*The cold, crisp air carried whiffs of pungent wood smoke and the calls of birds sounded clearly. There was just enough snow for a Christmas card effect, as bright lights sparkled from trees and windows. What better setting for the season of good will to men?*
                                                                               1985

From 1980:

*...On Wednesday and Thursday Randolph Center's famous winds tore across the hilltop without letup. Temperatures dropped below zero, while winds kept gusting more than 40 mph, producing chill factors as low as minus 45 degrees. It was bitter weather, best for staying close to home fires, and appreciating the benefits of four snug walls.*

*At the end of sunny days, trees on the horizon stand like a black ruff against the pale gold of the sky, their beauty stark and simple.*

On signs of winter from 1984:

*Sometimes the first lasting Vermont snowfall comes as early as October, or more commonly in November, but this year it did not happen until December...*

*The pungent smell of wood smoke is wafted to our nostrils on the crisp cold air, and warmth becomes our prime concern as bitter winds blow.*

From 1987:

*The white ground covering gave a wintry look to the landscape, and sparkling Christmas lights added cheer to the long nights which blanketed us early and late.*

*Snug against the blustering wind, homes assumed greater importance as we chose the course of resistance to winter, rather than the alternatives of wild creatures - hibernation or migration.*

On the "battle" against winter, from 1989:

*Bitter was the word generally applicable to the weather, with the mercury falling early on Thursday. Cracks and crevices, which used to be chinked with moss in the early days, were filled to conserve precious heat. In the long, dark hours of night, Jack Frost could be heard, "pulling nails," contracting in the cold.*

*There was comfort in the knowledge that daily sunlight would be increasing in only ten more days. Meanwhile, holiday lights and Christmas music brightened spirits, as the battle against Old Man Winter was being waged in earnest.*

December 14-20:

*Living with Vermont weather can be likened to the marriage vows-"For better, for worse... in sickness and in health!"*

*We know that the elements are going to try our souls with treacherous traveling, icy blasts and an assortment of ills. But just as surely, we know that beneath the frozen white expanse lie the dormant beginnings of next spring's tender beauty. And so we accept the wide variation in seasons with reasonable equanimity, and a touch of humor.*

*Last Tuesday was one of those days combining rain, snow and freezing rain after a pleasant morning. Wednesday featured powerful winds blowing incessantly, while Sunday was our first below-zero day.* 1983

Approaching the longest night from 1980:
*On clear nights, the crescent moon shines like an ornament pinned to the dark sky, as the longest night of the year approaches.*

From 1986:
*Trees formed wind-tossed silhouettes against a flaming sunset Wednesday afternoon. By evening, wind speed had reached a fearful 60 mph.*

*Friday's pearl gray skies hinted of snow. That night winter really sank its teeth in, as temperatures plunged toward zero. Heavy frost patterns on windows wavered like moiré taffeta...*

*As the year approached its darkest point, our hearts were gladdened by the joy of Christmas coming, and the knowledge that sunnier days lay ahead.*

One of the coldest Decembers on record continued in 1989:
*The theme of last week's weather was one of unrelenting cold, day and night. But sunshine every day except Saturday made the frigidity more bearable. Like cats gravitating to sunny spots, we sought warmth wherever we could find it.*

*The full moon shone majestically over broad expanses of white hills, while Orion waged his age-old battle with Taurus in the southern skies....*

*Thus far we have broken existing records for coldest December, and official winter hasn't even opened its bag of tricks yet!*

Surveying the environment in mid-December, 1994:
*Tattered remnants of brown oak leaves clung to sturdy trees, and field mice, alas, sought refuge in the warmth of houses. Flocks of goldfinches, juncos and tree sparrows joined regular guests at nearby feeding grounds.*

*Hours of daylight were few and precious, and darkness ruled the world early and late. It was the nadir of the year, a time of stillness and inactivity in nature, a time for contemplation and reassessment in our lives.*

*Across the miles of snow, warm wishes for peace and good will went out to all this Christmastime.*

December 21- 27:
*Clearly there is no such thing as typical Christmas weather in 13 years of Weatherwise observations. This year's holiday was a white one, but such has not always been the case. Last year, for instance, was bare, while in 1989, the cold-record-setting month, it warmed up to above zero.*

*In 1986 there was freezing rain, but shades of Rudolph - 1987 had fog! 1984 Christmas was distinguished by 57 mph winds, and in 1982 the wind velocity reached 62 mph. 1980 Christmas set a cold record of -34 degrees; 1979 had been green and rainy and in 1978 18 inches of snow fell.*

*All of which goes to illustrate that famous remark about New England weather, "If you don't like it, just wait five minutes!" And so we wait for next year's weather, confident that the sun will brighten more days than not.* 1992

More on that bitter cold Christmas Day from 1980:

*Not only was Christmas day the coldest on record, but also the lowest temperature ever recorded in the 30 years this weather observer has lived in Randolph Center. Thermometers plunged almost 60 degrees from Wednesday afternoon to Thursday morning's minus 34 degrees.*

*Winds of more than 30 mph created astonishingly low chill factors-sometimes minus 75 to 80 degrees!.....Old Man Winter may have won one battle, but we shall overcome!*

Mim noted the winter solstice from her December 26, 1985 column:

*Saturday, the winter solstice, traditionally was a time of rejoicing that there would be (more) light each day until the summer solstice in June. And that is still a good way for us to regard this turning point, when the bulk of winter lies ahead!*

Hurricane force winds were recorded on December 26, 1993:

*FLASH! Hurricane force winds were recorded Sunday PM by the Herwig anemometer for the first time in 15 years of operation. Previously there had been only one reading of 72 mph on December 7, 1989, and hurricane velocity is 75 mph and over. As gusts buffeted the house, readings in the 50's and 60's were common, until 80 mph was registered.*

*To put this into perspective - last year had only one reading of over 50 mph, while 1993 had only four such readings before Sunday. December 26, 1993 will be a day remembered!*

December 25-31, the year concludes:

*By last Monday morning, rain had disposed of most of our snow covering, bitter winds were howling and temps were dropping. Christmas Day dawned sunny and pleasant, but definitely not white. Wednesday's temperature went downward and the wind speed went upward.*

*Contracting nails popped explosively in Thursday morning's frigid air and Friday brought 2 ½" inches of fluffy snow. Rain, freezing rain, amazing warmth, and fog were the weekend story.*

*As 1990 draws to a close, it leaves behind memories of a very wet year which produced prodigious crops of flowers and vegetables as well as torrential rains in July and August. There were two 15" snowfalls, on Jan. 30 and March 20, and the highest wind speed was 62 mph on February 17. The first killing frost held off until October 17 here. Indian summer occurred early in November.*

*It was a good year for sugaring, and for living in Vermont.* 1990

From the last week of 1981:

*Packed white roads with banks of snow already high are reminiscent of "one-horse open sleigh" days. Snow fell on three days last week, balanced by three dazzlingly sunny days. And always lurking behind the next hill was that great snow sculptor, the wind.*

*The New Year came in 30 degrees warmer than last year's 15 below zero, and during the night wind velocity reached 48 mph. There is no doubt about the old-fashioned winter we are having.*

*"The woods are lovely, dark and deep,"[32] with the silent beauty of snow-decked evergreens broken only by the occasional flight of blue jays.*

From Mim's late December, 1982 column:

*"Here is an interesting account from the December 27, 1877 Herald and News: 'The weather is indeed remarkable for this time of year. On Christmas day the boys played ball and the air was warm and mild as in September. The oldest inhabitant is at a loss to account for such fine weather. But when shall we have winter?'"*

From the end of the century, December 30, 1999:

*...with the new millennium, Mim promises to keep a weather eye on our weather in Randolph Center. When all the figures are in, the last year of the 20th century may well have whirled off into history as the hottest on record worldwide.*

*For our part, the governor declared the whole state a disaster area, after three months of drought had parched the land. With the exception of October, every month had been warmer than average. Week after week there was no rain, and temperatures sky-rocketed.*

*Then in September, the backlash of Hurricane Floyd walloped us with more precipitation than had fallen in the previous three months. Flooding and high winds wreaked havoc during one memorable night.*

*Wind readings had been remarkably mild all year, with only two topping 50 mph. Why, 10 years ago, we had 15 60-mph readings!*

*Now we look forward to a new year filled with the mystery and majesty of Vermont weather.[33]*

---

[32]*Stopping by Woods on a Snowy Evening,* Robert Frost

[33]*Editor's parting note: Ironically as I conclude with the second round of editing of this book, I have been speaking with Mim on what may be our greatest snowstorm ever in a 24 hour period. The Valentine's Day blizzard of 2007 is still dumping snow late in the day with a total of 30.5 inches in less than 24 hours. The accumulation from this powerful nor'easter has doubled our total for the entire winter to date. Such can be the way of weather in Vermont. And so the two of us complete this volume as we continue our mutual "Love Affair with Vermont Weather."*

# Acknowledgements

This project never would have happened without the strong and continuous support of my wife Ellen, who carried extra duties at home whenever I was working on this book. Of course I also wish to thank Mim Herwig; not only has it been a pleasure to work with her, but I will always treasure all those times in her kitchen, talking about the weather, history and the changing times, both here in Randolph and throughout the State of Vermont. Her eighth generation sense, along with her engaging wit and wisdom has served as a personal inspiration to me, both in continuing her weekly column, and in my own personal pursuit of the study and writing of local history.

I am also indebted to Vermont historian and noted Civil War writer Howard Coffin, who as my first real editor, filled my initial draft with plenty of red ink, while simultaneously encouraging me with the positive feedback I needed at that point, stating that this was no more than the level of edits that his editors often gave to him. Further proof reading and edits were provided by author and radio commentator Charles Morrissey - they came at a time when I was ready to finish, but they proved invaluable in steering this project towards its ultimate conclusion. For any mistakes remaining I alone remain responsible. By no accident and through Mim's suggestion, we ended up working with Bill Sharp of Sharp and Company Printers, and his suggestions on putting this all together at the end were invaluable - Bill himself is extremely interested in Vermont weather and is a National Weather Service Cooperative Observer in Rutland. His late father worked many years with both Wes and Mim Herwig previously on many of their local and Vermont history books. I also want to thank Larry Patin from Sharp and Company Printers, for his helpful suggestions and work during the final editing process.

Bert Moffatt also deserves credit, both for his support of this endeavor and for his introduction of Nancy Stone's beautiful art work that graces these pages. I consider myself fortunate to have forged a friendship with Bert, who as long time local town manager here had already developed a long lasting relationship with the Herwig family which endures to this day. Of course I greatly appreciate, and wish to acknowledge the artist Nancy Stone, for her incredibly generous donation of the reproductions of her unique and special portrayals of the Vermont seasons - certainly it was no accident that through Bert and some good timing we were able to "marry" these prints with the prose that Mim brought to the pages of The Herald. I also wish to thank Mim's granddaughter, Crystal Roberts, for her concept of the book's cover design.

*Other family members deserve thanks including my children, Geoffrey and Elissa for their patience when "Papa" was at work on the computer, (Geoffrey also provided the drawing of the flower seen before the month of June) and more recently our new family member and year long visiting student from Germany, Tobias Nielsen, who brings a remarkable passion to photography and who helped with several of the photographs found within this book. I provided the January and October photographs taken in Randolph Center, while credit for the April picture goes to the late Wes Herwig, taken at the home he shared with Mim and his family for over 50 years here in the Center. The beautiful lilac photograph was taken by Mike Chaloux, who also works at Sharp and Company Printers.*

*Finally, on a personal note, I would like to thank God for orchestrating our move to Randolph Center, Vermont, the exact location where I could best exercise my passion for tracking the weather and completing this project with Mim.*

*Kevin Doering,*
*Randolph Center, Vermont - October 24, 2007*

# About the Author

Mim Herwig is an eighth generation Vermonter who grew up on a small farm blessed with an abundance of weather. She and her late husband, Wes, published 40 books and shared an intense interest in history. She is a charter member and past President of the Randolph Historical Society.

Mim records weather history and wrote the weekly column "Weatherwise", printed in the The Herald of Randolph from 1978 - 2003. She has five daughters, seven grandchildren and three great-grandchildren and resides in a beautiful Greek-Revival home in historic Randolph Center, Vermont.

# About the Editor

Kevin Doering is a meteorologist, journalist, amateur photographer and environmental health practitioner who lives with his wife Ellen and their two children, Geoffrey and Elissa, in an historic home in Randolph Center, Vermont where he still heats and occasionally cooks with wood. He has authored the weekly column, "Weatherwise" for The Herald of Randolph since October, 2003.

# About the Illustrator

*(Paintings for February, March, July, August, September, November, December & Covers)*

Nancy Stone is a painter, book artist and art teacher. She is a member of the Northern Vermont Artists Association, the Bryan Memorial Gallery in Jeffersonville and a Signature member of the Vermont Watercolor Society. Her acrylic and watercolor paintings have received numerous awards, including 2005's "Juror's Choice" top award at the Vermont Watercolor Society and "Grand Prize" (Enterprise Corp. pick) at the Champlain Valley Exposition. Her hand-made artist's books have been in juried shows at the Wood Art Gallery, Montpelier, and Studio Place Arts Gallery, Barre; one book received the Juror's Award at the Shelburne Art Center/Book Arts Guild show. In the Burlington area, Nancy taught art at Williston Central School for twenty-one years; she is Co-Founder/Co-Chair of the Vermont Book Arts Guild, teaches "Introduction to Book Arts" at the Community College of Vermont, and mentors young artists.